Surviving Cambodia
The Khmer Rouge Regime

WRITTEN BY

BUN T. LIM

PUBLISHED BY

TRAFFORD
USA • Canada • UK • Ireland

© Copyright 2006 Bun T. Lim

All rights reserved. No part of this publication may be reproduced, stored in a retrieval system, or transmitted, in any form or by any means, electronic, mechanical, photocopying, recording, or otherwise, without the written prior permission of the author.

Note for Librarians: A cataloguing record for this book is available from Library and Archives Canada at www.collectionscanada.ca/amicus/index-e.html

ISBN 1-4251-1285-4

Completed February 17, 2005

Printed in Victoria, BC, Canada. Printed on paper with minimum 30% recycled fibre.
Trafford's print shop runs on "green energy" from solar, wind and other environmentally-friendly power sources.

TRAFFORD
PUBLISHING

Offices in Canada, USA, Ireland and UK

Book sales for North America and international:
Trafford Publishing, 6E–2333 Government St.,
Victoria, BC V8T 4P4 CANADA
phone 250 383 6864 (toll-free 1 888 232 4444)
fax 250 383 6804; email to orders@trafford.com

Book sales in Europe:
Trafford Publishing (UK) Limited, 9 Park End Street, 2nd Floor
Oxford, UK OX1 1HH UNITED KINGDOM
phone 44 (0)1865 722 113 (local rate 0845 230 9601)
facsimile 44 (0)1865 722 868; info.uk@trafford.com

Order online at:
trafford.com/06-3044

10 9 8 7 6 5 4 3 2

I would like to dedicate this book to my mother who raised the three of us with love, compassion, dignity and pride. She was the foundation of our family, and we will honor her by carrying on her legacy the way she would wish. My mother passed away unexpectedly on February 17, 2005. She went through a lot in her lifetime, but she always lived her life to the fullest. She remained strong until her very last day. My mother (KIM HEAK LIM) was the reason why the four of us made it here to America. She was the strongest and most compassionate woman I ever knew. She lost her husband and many of her relatives during the Khmer Rouge Regime, but she managed to survive the ruthlessness of the Khmer rouge and held on to her three children, my sister Amanda (Bunsay) Lim, myself (Bunthong) Lim and my brother (Bunpa) Lim. She helped all three of us survive Cambodia and the Khmer Rouge during those difficult times in the 1970's.

After my father was killed during the Khmer Rouge Regime, my mother devoted her life to her three kids. She often told all of us that we were her life and she meant every word she said. She never remarried and made many sacrifices in order to bring all three of us to America with the help of my uncle, her older brother, the only brother she had who is still alive. My mother was both a father and a mother to all three of us, and she did it better than most parents. My mother taught us the values of love, life and devotion. Even though she had left us physically, she will always be with us in our hearts, minds and souls.

We would like to also say thank you to my special uncle who sponsored all of us to come to America for a better life. My uncle is a very quiet but intelligent man, and, along with my mother, he is the reason why we are all here in America today. We owe him a great deal. We appreciate all that he has done for us, more than he will ever know, and we will forever be grateful!

Introduction:

Surviving Cambodia, The Khmer Rouge Regime.

My name is Bunthong Lim. I was born in Cambodia January 1st, 1967. This story is about me and my family, the struggle we went through during the Khmer Rouge Regime, and how fortunate we were to have escaped from Cambodia. I thought about writing this story for a long time but never had the time to do it because of school and work. After thoroughly thinking this through, I realized it meant a lot for me to write about my struggle and my family's struggle during the Khmer Rouge regime.

It hurts me to write this story because it brings back bad memories, but I feel that I have to do it for my own record and reference. I also want to share this with everyone who's interested. We were an upper class family in Cambodia. My father was an educated man and the principal of a High School; his passion was to help young students achieve their educational goals. My father was a soft-spoken man who loved his family and all his kids very much. My mother owned a couple of clothing/jewelry shops, which she ran by herself. Occasionally her cousins would help out. We were living in Phnom Penh, the city of my birth.

My sister and I were young students during the early 1970's. We would go to school each day dressed in a school uniforms to get an early education while mom and dad worked to provide for all of us. I also had a young brother who was still too young to go to school, so my mother and father had a maid look after him while they were at work and my sister and I were in school. Since she is the oldest of the three of us, my sister would help my mom and dad and the maid take care of my brother and me. Even though I was still a young boy, I knew that life was great in Cambodia before the Khmer Rouge took over.

I was around 5 or 6 years old, my father used to wake us all up early, dress all of us up and take us to breakfast at the market. We could have whatever we wanted, and often we would have Cambodian noodle soup, soup rice or steamed chicken over garlic rice with fish sauce mix, lemon and green onion, one of my favorite dishes in the morning back then. All the food was cooked fresh right there in front of us as we waited to eat. The food was so good everywhere. We could just pick a spot in the market, sit down and eat fresh food cooked in front of us.

Afterward, my dad would bring us all out to walk in the park so we could enjoy the sunny day. Cambodia had so many wonderful and beautiful parks and gardens filled with exotic flowers and trees. I believe my father wanted us to see the beauty of our country and its landscape.

I remember the good times I spent with my father, mother,

sister and then very young baby brother before the Khmer Rouge took over our country. We lived a wonderful and happy life and had a father and mother who loved and cared a lot about all of us. They wanted us to have a good education, morals and values. My mom and dad worked hard to provide for all of us, making sure we were never short of anything. However, things changed rather quickly when the Khmer Rouge, also known as "The Red Cambodians," took over on April 17, 1975. I will do my very best to recollect and tell you the story about my life and my family's life as we struggled to survived the Horror of "The Red Cambodians".

Chapter 1

April 17, 1975: the date forever changed our lives and the country we dearly loved, Cambodia. I woke up to loud explosions, gunfire and people yelling and screaming. My mom and dad gathered all of us to one place in the house, so we would not be scattered. There were adults and young teenagers, probably not much older than myself, pointing guns and grenades at us outside of our home and ordering us to leave the house immediately. They also told us not to take anything with us because we all would return home soon. This was not true!

These people that forced us out of our own home were part of the Khmer Rouge; all were wearing a red and white, checkered bandanas. It was a part of their ritual. On this day my mom and dad had just enough time to gather the family, some clothes and a few important things, such as pictures of us; we left everything else at home, hoping that we all might be back home soon!

We all got in the car, and soon were on the road, leaving our home behind, traveling along with everyone else who was also forced out of their homes. The streets were so full of people, cars, motorcycles, mopeds and cyclos that there was barely any room to drive the car.

Would you like to know what a cyclo is? I will try my best to explain it to you. Basically it is like a big version of a reverse tricycle, except you can fit two persons in the front seat and one in the back to pedal the bike. Cyclos are used as taxis to carry people from one place to another around town. The person that sat on the single seat in the back would be the one to pedal the cyclo.

The streets were hot, and dusty. Everyone was screaming and yelling, and babies were crying; it was terrible!

The Khmer Rouge wanted to force us out to the countryside so they could get control of all of us city people and also control the country. These people do not like an educated person or wanted any part of it. Actually, if they find out that you are educated or have any education at all, they will take you out and kill you. For this reason we will never understood their purpose. These red Cambodians worked under the main leader called Pol Pot, who ran the whole army, called The Khmer Rouge: He "Pol Pot" brain washed these people and young teenagers, trained them to torture and murder innocent people with no remorse. You will see what I mean as I continue my story.

We were led to believe that we would be coming back to our home in a couple of days as we fled our home together with everyone else. The streets of Phnom Penh were filled with scared and angry adults and children as we continued our way out of the city. As we got farther away from the city, we realized that we were not going to be able to continue driving the car because there were too many people on the street. We left the car and continued our journey to the countryside on foot like everyone else. My mom and dad left the car in the middle of nowhere; they had no other choice.

We continued to walk for many miles, until the sun started to set. The day became evening, and everyone was stopping for a rest in the middle of a small town. We were all so exhausted and hungry that we decided to crash out first and think of food after we got a little rest. We also had our grandmother with us, and she was still strong, keeping up with all of us pretty well as we continued our way. We all did not know where we were going or when we were going to stop for good. We just followed the crowd of people as we were told time after time.

We stopped at this little town and got some rest. We were all hungry now, and it was time to look for food around town. We brought some rice with us, but it was not enough. I remember people were killing pigs and chickens left and right so they could have something to eat. I don't remember if we killed any pig or chicken in that town, but I do remember we had some roast pork that people had cooked, and they gave us some to eat.

All the vegetables in this town were picked by other people and by all of us because we needed something to eat; we were very hungry. After we had food and everyone had settled down to sleep for the night in this little town, people were lying around everywhere they could find a spot to sleep. There were so many adults and children everywhere, we were all fearful of not knowing what was going to happen next.

Some of the killings had already started as we were all sleeping. The sound of gunfire continued throughout the day and night. We all just tried to stay as close to each other as possible, so none of us would get lost or be taken away. The next morning we continued to walk and follow the herds of people, who were all moving in the same direction. My younger brother was still a baby then, so my mom and dad took turns carrying him as we all continued to walk to our unknown destiny.

Soon, we all had to stop again for another rest at another town when everyone else decided to stop too; it was safer when we stopped with everyone as a group--at least we knew someone else was with us at all times. It was a dangerous situation, not knowing where we were at or where we were going. We were all scared, but at the same time, we tried to be optimistic.

We were trying to find another spot to sit down and rest together so we would have energy to continue the next day. Evening time came again as we found a spot next to this older lady lying there fast asleep by herself. We thought this would be a great place to rest, since she was alone and had no one with her. There would be enough room for all of us there too. As we woke up the next morning, the lady was still sleeping next to us; I think it was next to my mom or grandmother. Something doesn't seem right with her; she could not have slept that much with out moving around. We later discovered that the old lady had been dead for quite sometime. We guessed she probably died from starvation the day before. This was the first of many scary things I witnessed.

Chapter 2

We all left this area very quickly and found another place to stay for a short time before we had to go again as the sun came up in the morning. I remember walking to the close by river to look for water to drink and wash up before we left this place. As I got closer to the river, I saw something very large and unusual looking floating slowly on the water's surface. I thought it was a big dead fish or a log floating on the river, but as it got closer to me I realized it was a dead human, swollen to three times the size of a regular person; it was very scary looking and it smelled terrible.

I ran back quickly to let my mom and dad know about this dead person floating on the river. Someone had either killed this person or he may have slipped down to the river and drowned. I never went close to the river again because of this reason and also because I did not know how to swim. My mother and father had warned me not to ever leave their sight and never go close to the river again, as it is very dangerous. My mother and father told me there might be a lot more dead people floating around the river.

I was so scared that I never wanted to go near the river by

myself ever again. We resumed our journey, as everyone was leaving this small town at the same time; it was like herds of animals. When one left, everyone else left too, because we were all scared for our lives and didn't know what would happened if we didn't follow the crowds of people.

As we continued each day, our bodies becomes weaker, and we all lost weight because there was not enough food to eat. I remember feeling very sad as we move through one little town after another for many reasons: There were yelling and screaming children, gun shots were fired continuously, and people ordered us to stay in one group, like animals, as we moved forward. Even though I was a young boy, I knew then that nothing good would come out of this. We tried hard to stay together, as we moved step-by-step forward with other people from place to place. We knew if we lost each other we would be in big trouble and probably would not find each other again.

People walked shoulder to shoulder all over the street. As we walked farther and farther each day, we saw fewer people moving forward with us, or should I say there were fewer crowded people moving forward. By this time, I believe The Khmer Rouge had ordered some of the people to go separate ways or toward a different area. That's all we know.

By this time the streets became less crowded, and it was a little easier to move forward as we had more room. There were always fears and doubts in our minds as we kept on moving forward: are they going to shoot us? Are they going to kidnap us and take us all away somewhere? Are they going to torture us because we are from the city? We did not know what would happen the next minute. I have said it earlier that the killing already started; it was very true!

We had seen dead people on the streets with gunshot wounds to the heads and bodies as we fearfully walked past them. To an eight-year-old kid, seeing dead people on the streets, floating on water swollen up to the point they were unrecognizable, it was very traumatic.

The worst was yet to come! Even though we saw dead people on the streets, we had to pretend that we didn't see it at all and kept on moving because we were very scared to stop and look at the dead people, knowing that we might be next if we were to stop and cause a scene of some sort. These Khmer Rouge people were cruel and would kill you right away if you didn't follow there orders precisely.

We knew at this time that our lives were in danger, and we needed to be very careful of what we said, in case any Khmer Rouge were nearby. The dead people that we walked past probably said something or did not follow their orders, or maybe the Khmer Rouge just didn't like them and decided to end their lives.

Every now and then Khmer Rouge soldiers would walk past us and with their guns pointing up in the air, yelling "move on" with a mean look in their eyes that said they would kill if their orders were not followed. By this time, we realized that going back home in a couple of days would not happen, and we probably would never see our home again. Within just a few days our lives had been turned upside down, from having everything and living comfortably to having to search for food in an area we were not familiar with. Young adults and teenagers who were carrying guns and grenades were controlling us; they took us to wherever they wanted.

The nightmares now had begun and we were all in it together. My father, my mother, sister, brother, grandmother and uncle, we were all together at this point. We had other family members, like cousins, nieces, nephews and other uncles that were separated from us from the beginning when The Khmer Rouge forced us out of our house.

We did not have time to gather other family members who lived by us. At this time they all probably were forced to a different area than we were. We all left our house as quickly as we possibly could to avoid getting shot at by The Khmer Rouge.

We were now getting closer to the countryside as we prepared to stop again for the night in this wide-open area with many big mango trees. We were now about four days away from Phnom Penh. We found another place to stay for the night as the evening came around and the sun was setting.

Before sunset, we walked around in search of food and discovered some new areas. This countryside seemed to be so empty, like no one had lived there before. Everything around there was like a wrecking yard, and it looked like people had been through there before searching around like we were. As we wandered through this area of town and looked at each mango tree in search for some left over fruits, we came to a big tree with big branches hanging down. As I turned around to look at the other side of the tree, I saw a dead man hanging from one of the branches by what I thought was a towel-like material, maybe a long sarong. We turned around and ran from this place as fast as we could to get away from the dead man. We were all terrified, not knowing if we might meet the Khmer Rouge on our way back to our resting area.

Seeing a dead man hanging from the tree was very disturbing to me. I often feel very confused and sad because I did not know why all of a sudden we started to see dead people in different places, nor did I have the time to ask why this was happening. We all pretended like we didn't see anything at all as we got back to our own area.

We were afraid to say anything to anybody about what we had seen. If the Khmer Rouge knew about what we had seen, we would be in danger for sure.

Knowing we were no longer safe anywhere, we did not sleep well that night. Furthermore, we were unsure where we would end up at the next day. Everyone around us felt exactly the same way as we all gathered around to get ready to move on the next day. We moved along with other people and came to this place in the countryside where we were told by the Khmer Rouge we would have to stay and get used to it. The voices of these red Cambodians as they spoke to us (or I put it yelled at us) with guns and rifles pointing directly at us put fear in our minds. We did exactly what they said and would not even think of asking any questions because if we did ask it might be our last.

As we settled down in this new area and tried to look for any food for ourselves, it became apparent that we were going to struggle to stay alive. Nobody cared what we needed to do to survive. We simply had to find whatever we could to eat, whether it would be fruits or vegetables or meat.

This was all very new to us. We didn't have to search for food before. We came from the city, and life was very different; if we wanted food, we took money and went to the market to buy food, and it worked out great. We did not know how to survive outside the city, including what to do if we did not have the money for food. We had to make an adjustment, and our minds thought differently in order to have a chance at surviving.

We were put in this situation without any warning whatsoever. Now here we were in unfamiliar territory, and we all have to do what it took to survive. The Khmer Rouge now had control over us and could do whatever they wanted at anytime. We were not used to, being controlled by people with deadly assault weapons.

At this time we knew a couple of things about The Khmer Rouge, or "Red Cambodians." For example, they did not like anybody with an education and they did not like anybody who asked too many questions or did not follow their orders. If they found out that you had an education or asked too many questions and not followed their orders, they would not hesitate to take you out, and that was their promised to all of us. We knew this much is true.

Somehow The Khmer Rouge, led by their leader "Pol Pot," had been brainwashed to believe that education or educated people were not good. They wanted to eliminate educated people first and then whoever irritated them next. I believe Pol Pot wanted to take over the country and run it with people who had no education. It would be a lot easier for Pol Pot to run the country. Pol Pot was a cruel man, much like Hitler. To me he was more dangerous than Hitler.

We had been placed in this part of the country not by choice with other families that also came together with us or were forced here. This was the first area we settled in, as they wanted us to. We had no choice but to agree to it and say nothing. As I remember, this place wasn't that bad. We just had to search for food our own way in any way that we could. That was not easy to do since there wasn't much food to be had.

In the beginning, it was very challenging for all of us to gathered food for ourselves, since no food was offered to us by anybody, and we were too afraid to ask for food. So we stayed in this little hut as a family and hunted for food and searched for water each day to keep ourselves alive.

My father and I found this little embankment that lead to a pond where water flowed from a small river and we rested there; we were glad to have found it. The water looked clean enough to drink and fish, frogs and other reptiles possibly lived in the pond. This was great news to us because it meant we found food and water to live on for a while.

Each morning I would watch my father come down to this pond to get water and take it back to our hut and dump it onto this cement oval container that probably held at least 100 gallons. He would use two metal containers, each one tied by a string about three feet long and hooked onto each end of a piece of two-by-four-like wood, which was about five feet long. This was the tool my father would use to go down to the pond and get water for us.

This tool was homemade and would be strong enough to hold the two metal containers/buckets, which held about 7 gallons of water each. My father would put the two by four on his shoulders with the metal container hanging on each end; he used these containers to go down to the pond to get water for us every morning. This certainly was hard work my father had to do.

This was not an easy task. As I mentioned before, there was an embankment leading to the pond, and it was pretty steep. There was also a long and wide wooden ladder built on the embankment for us to use to go down to the pond to get water. I watched my father struggle to carry water with these two metal containers on his shoulders using the wooden stepladder. Sometimes he would slip from the ladder and fall back down to the pond and had to start over again. It was agonizing watching him do this every morning. I felt terrible that my father had to do this for us.

My father was a High School principal, and, until this time, he never had to work hard physically in his life. This was a new situation for him, and he had to make many changes that he was not used to.

We would also go fishing in this little pond for fish, crabs and frogs. Sometimes we caught a lot, and sometimes we caught less, depending on the day; we lived that way every day.

After awhile we became good at hunting and gathering live food for ourselves, and we felt a little more comfortable. After watching my father and other people do this every day, I learned a few things. As a young boy I was very active, always curious about everything, and I felt comfortable and confident that I could help my father.

Even though I was a young boy, I was a quick learner. So from this point on I would help my father get the water every morning, using the same method as my father, except I use smaller water containers, since I was just a kid.

I would help out gathering food and other goods, like fruits and vegetables and sometimes dry tree branches for starting fires, since we have no stove. Other people that were staying in the same place struggled to perform the same task each day. Hunting for live animals each day was a difficult task for many people.

By this time we had all lost some weight due to a lack of vitamins in our food, but we were surviving. We did not know how long we could survive this way; all we knew was we had to keep going, to stay together as long as we could and to maintain a positive attitude. All we had was each other and the mindset that some day we would be free again. I guess the tough time made us stronger and more independent.

After getting used to hunting and picking fruits and vegetables, we felt like we could go out in the woods and hunt for anything because we were more confident in our ability to hunt for ourselves.

Chapter 3

We had been ordered to stay put, keep our mouth shut, and do whatever they told us to. This meant if they wanted to move us to a different area or separate us they would do so whenever they like. We were told that soon we all would have to go out in the wheat field and work from dawn to dusk planting or removing wheat from the fields every day. Some people would be selected to go do other things, like hauling hays and moving dirt from one area to another to form a walkway.

In the meantime, we all stayed put and waited to see what would happen next. One thing that really helped us was the weather. I remember it was always warm, even at night, and when it would rain, the rain was also warm. That was a very good thing.

Whenever it started to rain, we knew that there would be more opportunities to find food because frogs and other inhabitants come out to play. That's when we would catch them and that would be our dinner. It sounds really cruel, and it was cruel to hunt down every animals or amphibian that we saw and kill them for our dinner, but that was the only choice we had to stay alive.

We all were surviving and living day by day under these shacks that were made out of bamboo. The roofs were made out of coconut tree braches and leaves. I'm not so sure of the name of this place that we were staying; all I knew then was it gave us an opportunity to survive, and that was all we needed at the time.

Close by where we were staying there were lots of banana trees and other exotic fruit trees filled with fruits. Sometimes we would survive only on fruits for a while when we could not find anything else to hunt. We were very thankful that at least these fruit trees were available for us, even though I wasn't sure what these fruit trees were called, besides the bananas.

Actually we couldn't just go out there and pick fruit all the time; we had to sneak out at night to pick these fruits because there were landowners still around, and they did not like it when we picked their fruit trees. They knew we all were forced here from the city and were held in captivity by the Khmer Rouge and sometimes needed food very badly. At this point it didn't matter if the owner of the fruit trees liked it or not. We picked their fruit anyway, day and night or whenever we were hungry.

Some of these fruit tree owners were also forced out of their homes by the Red Cambodians, leaving us with a place to stay. All we wanted to do was survive whatever way we could. When your body is starving, your mind change the way you think and that was what had happened to all of us. We became almost like animals. "Kill or be killed".

We stayed in this little village for several days. The time had come, and everyone, including the children, was told to get ready to go to work in the wheat field from morning to evening time. So my father, mother, uncle, sister and myself all had to go to work in the wheat field, while my brother stayed in the village with my grandmother.

My grandmother was not forced to work in the wheat field because she was too old and weak. On the other hand, my younger brother was just a small child and would not be able to work yet, so he ended up staying with my grandmother while we all worked. The work was exhausting, and it took a lot out of us. We had to go in the wheat field and pull out all of the old wheat and replant new young wheat fielding its place.

The work was backbreaking and tiring. We were offered a lunch break during midday and they gave each of us a small bowl of soup rice and then they hurried us all back to work. When we got home in the evening time after the loaded work day with only a small bowl of soup rice offered in mid day lunch, each of us was offered another bowl of cooked white rice for dinner and that was all we were getting for the day. Whatever you wanted to go with your rice you had to find it yourself. There was some salt given at the lunch and dinnertime, but that's all we got with the soup rice. Aside from potential starvation, the lack of essential vitamins was a big problem. The Khmer Rouge was working us so hard that each person became like a zombie at the end of each day.

I remember the best thing that I ate while we were there was frogs; they were everywhere on the field and at the place we were staying. Another thing I really appreciated at the time was crabmeat, and sometimes we even ate snakes and crickets that we gathered.

Day-by-day, we all grew weaker and weaker, but we still had hope that somehow some way we all would survive through this horrible time (or as I put it, nightmare). While we were staying at this place we called our temporary home, we made the best of what was available to us at the time. Our lives were in danger each day, and we all lived in fear of the Khmer Rouge.

If for some reason the Khmer Rouge didn't like any one of us or felt that we were no use, they could take us out to be killed. Sometimes the Khmer Rouge would come at night in groups to take people out one by one and kill them. We would hear people talking later the next day that the reason they were taking these people out was because they complained that the work was too hard and that food too scarce. Sometimes they found out that some people had education background and they did not hesitate to take those people out.

Most of the killings happened at night time, but sometimes they happened during daytime too. There were a few times as I recall that the Khmer Rouge had come looking for me when I was sick and could not go to work during the day, and my mother had to stay home to take care of me. The Khmer Rouge found out my mother and I weren't out on the field, so they came rushing into our shelter/home asking for me specifically. I thought they were going to take me out and kill me right there and then. As they forced their way into our shelter, my mother was very worried about what these people were going to do with me.

My mother told them that I was sick and could not get out of the house to go to work in the field. I remember they were yelling and screaming and they wanted me out of the house. I was afraid that they were going to kill me. I recall my mother asking them to check on me, so they could see that I was really sick and not pretending. They did check me out and agreed to let me stay home for that day with my mother. As it turned out later, they only wanted my mother and me to go to work; that was a huge relief.

As a little kid I was pretty tough, but when four or five angry adults carrying guns and rifles were yelling at me, wanting me out of the house while I was sick, I feared for my life. These people would often come by everyone's place to check up on them to see if they were going to work each day. So there was no excuse whatsoever for not working out in the wheat fields unless you were really sick like I was.

Working in the wheat fields every day was horrible; there were leaches of all sizes all over the wheat fields, and sometimes we had to deal with water snakes. Everyday we work on the fields, leeches clung on to our legs and bodies, and we had to get rid of them before they got further into our bodies.

Some of the leeches were so small that they could force themselves right into our legs and bodies, and we would feel them digging into our skin; it hurt pretty badly. I was not scared of the big leeches, the ones we called buffalo leeches, but I was terrified of the small leeches because they could get into my body. I was mostly afraid they would get into my penis and through my body that way.

Several times the small leeches almost did go into my penis. It was difficult getting them when they started going inside the hole because they were so small; it was terrifying, and I was lucky to get them out before they got completely inside of me.

These are some of the things we all had to deal with while working out on the fields. There are many frightening occasions where we also had to deal with water snakes around us in the water, because they were everywhere, small and big. The water snakes were not poisonous, but they were still scary to me. I can still recall more than a few times where I came up from the field for a short break and met face to face with a snake on the walkway. I ran away so fast it felt like I was flying. That was how scared I was of snakes of any kind. It terrified me and still gives me nightmares.

We have been forced to stay in this area for about six months, and we continued to do whatever they (the Khmer Rouge) told us to do. All of us were now going through some major changes, especially in our appearances due to the lack of food, vitamins, freedom and happiness. The stress of being kept under control like birds in a cage was taking a serious turn on all of us. My father was getting so weak from being pushed to work so hard and not having enough to eat everyday that he could barely gather enough strength to go to work.

He was getting pretty sick and my mother was trying to take care of him at our shelter. The Khmer Rouge did not like what was happening to my father, and everyday they would keep an eye on him. They knew that my father was not faking the sickness. For some reason they wanted to know why my father was sick; it seemed so stupid to me. He was overworked and didn't have enough to eat. That's why he was getting sick. They still wanted him to go out on the wheat field and work regardless. So my father continued to go to work even though he was pretty sick.

Chapter 4

The Khmer Rouge did not like or want anyone to stay home, even if they were sick; they did not care at all. They commanded each one of us to work like a slave and they pushed us beyond our limit until our bodies could not take it anymore.

As I have said, people died on the field and some came home and died because they had been overworked. Some even died on the way home from being overworked on the wheat field.

Even though she did not have to work, my grandmother was also getting sick quite often due to her age and lack of food and vitamins. My mom had to take care of my father and grandmother at the same time. My father was in worse shape than my grandmother at this time.

He lost a great deal of weight from being overworked and getting sick at the same time. There were no doctors, nurses, or medicine available for the sick. We dealt with whatever we had and did not complain to avoid the wrath of the Khmer Rouge.

While my father and grandmother were sick, we were told again by the Khmer Rouge that we could no longer stay where we were. They did not give us a reason why they were moving us again other than just move as quickly as you can and shut up, and go back to work on the wheat fields as soon as you have settled down in your new place and found a shelter. We followed the Khmer Rouge again to a new and unfamiliar area. We were all lost and didn't care anymore. We did whatever they told us to do and kept our mouths shut; we figured it was best.

We were moved to a new area that was even closer to the new wheat fields and work area. My guess is that they were bringing in new people to the area where we had stayed. They wanted us to get out of the old place and move on. That was the Khmer Rouge way, moving us around all the time from one area to another without any warning. They kept everybody scattered around the country.

A few weeks passed, and my father was still sick, but was getting a little bit better as we all could see in his face and body. So even though my father was still sick, the Khmer Rouge continued to force him against his will to go back to work on the wheat field each day. The Khmer Rouge told my father if he could walk he could work.

My mother was very concerned about my father's well being and worried that he may not make it if he continued to go to work. My mother tried to explain this to the Khmer Rouge in charge, but it did not matter one bit. My father would have to work and that was it. Not even my father could argue with them. My father's health meant nothing to these heartless people.

The Khmer Rouge had control of everything, including how we felt emotionally and physically. I know I was very young at that time, but I remember a lot of the things that happened while we all were living there, all of the horrible and gruesome details of what these people did to innocent people who just wanted to live. If you became weak and complained, they would take you out and beat you to death and dump your body in this big hole with the rest of the dead ones.

I have seen and remember vividly the things they did to innocent people. I get very upset and disturbed sometimes while writing this, but I must stay calm and composed and finish my story.

More than several weeks had gone by and my father was still sick. After all how can you get better if you are sick and continue to work without taking care of yourself? That's what my father did; he went to work on the wheat field, pulling and planting wheat while he was sick.

My father was in no condition to work, but the Khmer Rouge didn't see it that way. Nothing would keep you away from slaving on the wheat field as long as you can walk. They made sure of that!

My mother tried to explain my father's condition to the Khmer Rouge many times; she even begged them to let my father stay home to recover from his sickness, but it was just a waste of time.

My father came home from work each day and told my mother that he was very concerned about his well-being and that he was getting weaker and weaker each day. The strength he once had was now gone and he felt exhausted all the time. He told my mother that he was not sure how long he could continue to work feeling like this. There wasn't much my mother or anybody could do to change this. My father still had to go back to work the next day or the Khmer Rouge would kill him.

My father was in a worst situation imaginable. He was still sick and there was no medicine, and on top of that he had to go back to work on the cold wheat field. He also did not have enough food to eat, and he lacked essential vitamins to keep his body strong, especially when he was sick.

My father sat down many times to explain the situation that he was in to my mother, and he told her that if anything ever happened to him, she should take good care of herself and the kids because that is all she should have left. My mother told us about this conversation that my father had with her, and we all understood it well.

My mother told my father not to worry about anything and take care of himself and be strong, that things would get better soon.

One day my father went to work, and we all had expected him to return home as usual, but he never did. That day my father went to work was the last time we all saw him. He never returned home from work and that made no sense to any of us; why would he just disappear? We all wanted an explanations and a reason why my father had not returned home from work like he normally did. My mother asked every one at the work area and the field, but no one said anything regarding my father's disappearance. No one had seen anything or had seen him at all that day. My mother asked the Khmer Rouge what had happened to her husband and why he was not coming home from work. This was not like my father. Surely somebody must have seen something going on, but no one said anything.

The Khmer Rouge told my mother that my father died and they took him away to dispose him somewhere. When my mother heard this, she went into a rage and she screamed and yelled at the Khmer Rouge and asked them why and how my father died? He went to work that morning; how could he have died?

My mother continued to ask the Khmer Rouge; if her husband did actually die on the wheat field, why didn't they take him home to us so we all could see him one last time? My mother asked how they could do this to us. If their own family member, like their wife or husband, had died, wouldn't they want to see them? My mother didn't care what she said to the Khmer Rouge anymore. All she cared about was that her husband was missing and she was told that he was dead. My mother didn't care if they were going to take her away and kill her too. All she wanted was an answer from the Khmer Rouge.

This was their reply back: He is already dead; there is no reason for you guys to see him. It is a waste of time; we took care of him for you. My mother continued to yell and scream at them and asked them how they would feel if one of their family members was dead and they were told couldn't see them at all because we took care of him for you and it would be a waste of time to see him or her. They would have no answer back for my mom.

My mother was very lucky that they did not take her out and kill her too when this happened. No one could talk that way to the Khmer Rouge because they would take you out, but when my mother lost my father that day, it did not matter to her. She let all her anger and rage out at them, and they did not take her out; she was very lucky that day.

We got no answer from the Khmer Rouge or anybody as to the reason why or how my father died, except that he did die and was taken away from us to be disposed of somewhere in the field. This was very devastating to all of us, especially to my mother. My mother and all of us felt that my father did not simply die, even though he was sick and weak; it was not possible.

He at least would want to come home and see all of us before he died or before something happened to him. I think that either the Khmer Rouge could not stand him being weak anymore and just took him away and killed him or they found out that my father was an educated man, and killed him for that reason. That is the only reasonable explanation we all could think.

One thing we were very thankful for was that the Khmer

Rouge for some odd reason did not want to kill my mother after all the yelling and screaming she did directly at them that very sad day. Normally, my mom would have been taken away immediately and killed without any question whatsoever, but I guess they didn't kill her because they thought she went through enough that day.

Maybe at that very instant my mother let out her anger and rage towards them, and the sorrow she felt affected them, so they decided to stop without taking further action. What a lucky woman my mother was at that time.

We lived and learned each day that we were living under their control. The Khmer Rouge was as heartless and brutal as human beings could be. I never really fully understood why did these people of our own race hated educated people so much and decided to take their lives without good reason. It didn't make any sense to me at all.

Because I was a young boy while all these things were happening to our country, it made me think a lot about people. Why did people hate other people so much? Why did people want to hurt other people? We all lived and breathed the same air, and we even came from the same country. I had to keep it to myself for so many years because all the things that happened to our country and us didn't make any sense. I know I was young and had to go through some terrible misfortunes, but the worst of it was that my mind was filled with what I called toxic information's about human beings and how they work.

I saw so many bad things happen to other human beings while living in what we all called the killing fields; all the unnecessary killings and the ways people were killed. The Khmer Rouge loved to torture and kill people. I saw dead people with their skulls busted open and left in the side of street. People hung on mango trees with gunshot wounds to the back of the heads. Innocent people were beaten to death and left on the street and on the field. Young infants died under mango trees and nobody cared enough to bury them. Sometimes the Khmer Rouge would kill people by tying them up and beating them in the back of the head with rifle or tree branches, and sometimes they would use foreign objects to kill people and then throw their bodies into a pre-dug pit. Mostly they would torture people first and then kill them, depending on their moods.

I knew my father was murdered by the Khmer Rouge. I pray that the way my father was killed was a quick death and that he didn't have to suffer long. That is the only way I know how to ease my mind regarding my father's death.

The way that we all received the news of my father's death and the Khmer Rouge's refusal to let us see him made us all feel that he was definitely murdered by these animals. We knew from this point on after my father was killed, any one of us could be next, and there would be no warnings. We were all together at this time: My mother, grandmother and one uncle who was my mother's youngest brother.

We all thought about a way to escape this place and away from the Khmer Rouge, but there were no opportunities. First of all, none of us knew what part of the country we were in. We just knew we were in the middle of somewhere. We did not know a way out of this part of the country that was in the middle of nowhere.

Even if we all had an opportunity to escape, we would most likely be caught by the Khmer Rouge and killed because they were everywhere, even at nighttime. They constantly watched everything that we did.

Chapter 5

Shortly after my father had been killed we were again forced to move to another area of the country and work at a different wheat field. They were working us to death and moving us around from one area to another just like slaves. While we were at this new area, they forced some of us, especially the older people, to plant rice on the field.

Some people were forced to gather hay into one area while some others were forced to remove dirt and mud from one area to another to form a walkway around the wheat field, which was much harder than working on the wheat field.

My grandmother was also getting sick due to lack of food and vitamins. Just getting old didn't help her either. So she was sent to an area that they called a hospital, but it wasn't really a hospital; it was just a place where she could stay with other sick people who were getting ready to die. My grandmother was in her late sixties.

My grandmother had to stay in the hospital with other sick helpless people. She was basically by herself, but we checked up on her any chance we got because the place where they put her in was really not too far from where we were staying, but far enough. If I have to guess, it was probably about five miles, because I was the one that had to visit her more often than other members of the family.

Most of the time I visited my grandmother in the hospital to give her soup rice that my mother had cooked up for her. The so-called hospital only gave her a small amount of soup rice twice a day, once in the morning and again at nighttime. That was not enough to keep her well and alive at all. There was no effective medicine to give to my grandmother except a little food, and some rest. We hoped that she would heal on her own.

After working on the wheat field all day long, we were all very tired. The Khmer Rouge forced us to plant wheat and remove dirt and mud, with little food to give us strength. We needed something extra besides the small amount of soup rice given to us twice a day. My mother would spend time in the evening cooking up some soup rice to be sent for my grandmother so she would have enough to eat and not starve to death in the hospital. I wasn't sure where my mother got the extra rice for my grandmother, but she had some hidden.

I think maybe she had traded other things that she had for the rice or she had stolen some from the wheat field in order to keep it at home. Anyway, it didn't matter how she got the rice; I'm just glad that she had some at home to cook. After the small meal they gave us in the evening, none of us were anywhere near being full, but it was all we had. A small amount of soup rice in a bowl with some salt to go with it and that's all for the night for everyone.

After we all had the meal, my mother would pack the soup rice that she made for my grandmother earlier in a silver container for me to take to my grandmother in the hospital. I remember that the soup rice that my mother cooked for my grandmother was much better than the soup rice the Khmer Rouge gave us. It was thicker and almost like rice instead of soup rice, if you know what I mean. So I was the designated person to deliver the soup rice to my grandmother in the hospital everyday. I guess my mother wanted me to do this because I was the older child and I was a quick learner and already knew the road to where my grandmother was.

I remember my first day of delivering the soup rice to my grandmother; I was so tired and scared that someone might steal the soup rice away from me on my way there because it was far away. Tired and all, I made it there through the wheat fields and rough terrain to delivered the soup rice for my grandmother. I felt so happy and proud that I got the food to my sick grandmother. I was a happy kid!

When I got to the hospital I notice that my grandmother had also been given some food from where she was staying. It was a bowl of semi-thick soup rice with some salt on the side. To me it was exciting to see food on the table at that time, and it didn't matter what kind of food as long as it was food; it could just be bones as far as I was concerned. Anything as long as it was food looked good to me. That was how amazingly starving hungry I was at the time.

So my grandmother had enough food to eat while she was in the hospital, including the food I brought for her personally. I will tell you a funny story from the second day on that I brought the food for my grandmother. I'm kind of embarrassed now to tell this, but I will do it for the sake of the book because it's all true.

My second day of delivering food and soup rice for my grandmother, I figured out that the only way for me to survive to continue doing this delivery of food everyday was to sit down somewhere quiet midway through the trip and chow down on some of the food and soup rice that my mother had prepared for just my grandmother.

Now I know that it was wrong to do that, but I had no other choices because I was so hungry, and a boy has to eat too to survive, especially when he has to perform extra duty. I ate perhaps 25 % of the food that I was to bring for my grandmother; I knew that if I ate more than that my mother would find out.

Sometimes I had to carry two very full containers of soup rice, and I mean full to the lid. That's how my mother would fill these containers each day for me to take to my grandmother, maybe she just wanted my grandmother to have leftovers too, and she did, just not as much or as often when I reached the hospital from the second day on. Basically, I just wanted to share the food with my grandmother. After all, I was the one to deliver food to her everyday.

I remember feeling excited to deliver the food again from the second day on, even though it was kind of far, and sometimes it would rain hard on my way there, and I had to struggle just to make it, but having to eat some of the food midway through my trip each day made it easier and gave me much more energy. I felt bad that I took a portion of my grandmother's food when it was specifically and especially made for her, but at that time I had to do what I had to do in order to make it back safely and do it again tomorrow as ordered by my mother.

I don't think my mother realized how starving hungry and tired I was. I have always thought to myself at least she should have made some extra soup rice for me too before sending me out to do an adult job. I worked very hard each day, and in the evening my other job was to deliver soup rice to my grandmother in the hospital. I just wanted to clarify that there were no doctor or nurses in this hospital. Like I said it wasn't really a hospital, more like a place for old people who were dying.

However, about a few weeks or so after my mother had visited my grandmother in the hospital herself to see how she was doing, she asked my grandmother, "did you have enough food to eat since the day of my delivering soup rice?" My grandmother told my mom yes the food was enough but asked my mother if the containers of soup rice she sent were always about 75% full and not completely full?

My mother replied: "Mom, the containers of soup rice that I sent to you have always been full to the lid."

Now at this time I knew I was in big trouble and had to find some way to deal with my mother. I had to find a way to tell her why the container of soup rice was not full when it got to my grandmother. When my mother returned from the hospital, she asked me all sorts of questions in regard to why the soup rice she sent with me to my grandmother was not full when it got to her each day?

My only answer to my mother that I could think of at the time was I fell down and part of the soup rice in the containers came out, and I was able to save the rest of it and delivered to grandma. I had lied to my mother, and it sounded good.

What a smart answer I thought that was at the time. Little did I know my mom asked me another question instead of feeling sorry for me that I fell down on my way there? Her next questions was, "did you fall down everyday on your way there, and is the soup rice that you've been able to save always exactly the same amount, which would be about 75% left in the containers?"

Now I was in deep trouble, and there were no good answer that could come out of this one. I finally had to tell my mother the truth, and it set me free even though my mother did not like my answer. My mother understood the reason why I had been eating a portion of my grandmother's soup rice. At least she knew I had to do it.

My delivering food days to my grandmother ended that day also. I was somewhat disappointed because now I couldn't have extra food anymore. My mother was doing the delivery herself from that day on. She also learned how difficult it was to deliver the food to my grandmother.

I went through a lot of trouble just to get the food to my grandmother, and I was tired by the time I got there. Remember, I was only a kid, but a tough one. After a few days of delivery, my mother finally felt sorry for me; she even mentioned it was difficult for her to do it. It made me feel I was appreciated.

Although grandma was getting enough food to eat, she was still not getting better. Her old age had taken a toll on her. She had more to eat than any of us at the time, while we all were pretty much starving.

At the time my mother really took great care of my grandmother, making sure that she was well fed each day. My mother took pride in doing this even in hard times. My mother was a brave woman.

Chapter 6

Meanwhile, my uncle who was my mom's youngest brother became sick also due to lack of food, nutrition and vitamins. He also had to be sent away to a nearby hospital, as they called it. My uncle was in that hospital for a long time because he wasn't getting any better.

We often visited him in the hospital and snuck in some food like we did with grandma, but it didn't help him much. My uncle became so sick that he was not able to take in much food at all. The problem was that there were no medications to help him, and when you became sick for so long without taking any medicine to help your body, it doesn't want to heal anymore. That was apparent in my uncle's case.

Your body rejects everything else you put in it. That was what's happening to my uncle. So while my uncle was very sick in the hospital, my grandmother passed away in a different hospital. My mother was devastated when she learned that my grandmother had passed away; she thought she had really taken good care of my grandmother, more than anybody else in the family.

My mother took excellent care of my grandmother since

the first day we were forced out of our home. She felt her mom should still be alive because she had plenty of food to eat, and she was not that sick at all. I thought my grandmother had died because of old age. It really hurt my mother when grandma passed away because she really loved her mom so much and took such good care of her through the year even though it was tough.

Food was hard to find, and time was limited due to the restrictions of the Khmer Rouge.

No matter how difficult it was to find extra food, my mother always found a way to get the rice and the time to get it to my grandmother, whether it was through me or doing it herself. She was a smart woman who always found a way when no one else could to survive, whatever it took.

Having to bury her mom in a small ditch that barely covered her body because there were no other spaces available really made my mother very sad. This is not what my mother wanted to do for her mom when she passed away. She wanted a nice funeral for her mother where she could come and visit her and bring nice flowers for her, but that wasn't going to happen as she was told she was lucky that her mom would be buried anywhere at all.

It was time to move on, and my mother didn't have any other choice but to do just that. We had now lost my father and grandmother in the same year, and my uncle was seriously sick in the hospital, and there were no treatments for him while he was there. This was the Khmer Rouge way; if you were sick you better pray that you will get better without any medicine to help you. If you don't get better, your chance of surviving was very slim to none.

A few weeks has gone by as we continued to visit my uncle in the hospital, and mom told him the news that grandmother had passed away. That made his condition worse than it was, but we had to tell him so he would know the truth. My mother had to do this. Keeping the truth away from my uncle was not what my mother wanted to do.

We watched my uncle's condition. He has gotten very skinny, just skin and bones. Than he swelled up like a balloon the next few days, and he looked horrible and scary. His skin became yellowish, and fluid started leaking out of his body when we touched him on his skin. Something bad had happened to my uncle. My mother started crying whenever we visited him, and he was not able to say much at all, just a few words at this time.

The words that I remember he said to my mother were; "take good care of all your kids. I'm not going to make it." He also told my mother that there was nothing she could do to help. This was all very traumatic to me, especially seeing all these things happening to my family and how my mother had to deal with it by herself without her husband and mother. We all saw how sick my uncle was. There was not a thing anybody could do to help him.

We knew that he was not going to make it, and that it was just a matter of time. My mother would stay with my uncle every day trying hard to keep him strong with encouraging words to fight and stay alive, but it didn't matter; he was just too sick. About a week later my uncle passed away, and again my mother had to bury him by herself. I'm not exactly sure where, but I think it was next to grandma. I may be wrong about this.

We were not sure what was going to happened next, but we knew that all we had now was the four of us: my mother, my sister, my brother, and myself, all trying to survive this horrible ordeal. I remember feeling very sorry for everyone because of all of the things that were happening to our family. I have often asked myself why these things happened and how come we couldn't stop it. I was afraid of what was going to happen with my life from that point on and what was going to happen to my family. So many bad things already happened to us, what was going to happen next?

A few months after my uncle had passed away, we were forced again to move to another area, and this time it was by the river. All I knew was we were somewhere in the middle of the country. That was good news to us because at least now we would have water to drink. Even if we were starving hungry, we could go down to the river and get water as a replacement. We were happy to be near the river! At least we had water and that was a big advantage.

The Khmer Rouge still were not giving us anymore food than we had before, just a bowl of soup rice with salt twice a day, and that was it. Beyond that, you were on your own. At this new place, there were many opportunities for us to stay alive. At least that was what we thought being near the river. We walked around and explored these new places and have found that there were areas where taro, red and green peppers, and lettuce grew. That was the best thing we saw since being forced out of our own home.

To all of us this new area of the country was a big improvement as far as surviving was concerned. While we were there, my mother thought of many ideas of how to survive. She had the courage to speak to the Khmer Rouge in regards to the problems that she was having with her heart. She told them that it was not beating regularly ever since she had lost her husband, mother and brother. "I'm having problem breathing," she continued.

She would beg the Khmer Rouge to have her stay home to take care of herself or maybe work on something else much lighter than working out on the wheat field. She explained that she could have a heart attack and die anytime if she overworked herself. She asked who would take care of her kids if she died; she had already lost her husband, mother and brother in the same year.

She continued to explain to them that it was too much for her to handle, and that was why she was having a heart condition right now. The amazing part of it was that they believed her, and I guess because there were no doctors to prove otherwise. So from that point on, while we were staying in this new part of the country, my mother was off the hook with the Khmer Rouge, and she no longer had to work on the wheat field. The Khmer Rouge gave mom a different job to do.

They told her to go to work at the pepper field, picking red and green peppers for the farmers closer to where we were staying. Picking peppers was much lighter work than working out on the wheat field, and that may have saved my mother's life.

Little did we know at the time that my mother did not really have a heart condition at all; she simply wanted to just stay away from the wheat fields. Working on the wheat fields was too much, especially if you did not have enough to eat each day; the workload alone could eventually kill you. So this was my mother's smart idea that she came up with in order to stay away from the work in the wheat field, and thank god it worked for her; she was lucky again. While living in this area of the country, life seemed to be a little better than it was in previous months; there was other food we could gather each day besides the soup rice.

We can go out after work and search for sweet potatoes, white taro, corn or sugar cane. This was something extra we could do to help ourselves survive; some people would do better than others in finding some of extra food, depending on their skill level, alertness and how far they wanted to.

My mother would come home with something extra, like a bag of taro or sweet potatoes and some green and red peppers, since she was working in the pepper fields. Since my father passed away, I felt like I needed to take the role of a man, even though I was just eight years old. My uncle also passed away, and the only person left in our family to fill the man's shoes would be me because my little brother was too small at the time to be productive.

So I took on more responsibility, gathering dead tree branches for the cooking fire. It sounded easy enough, but it wasn't because I sometimes had to wander into the deeper area of the country and sometimes into the jungle part of the country in order to find these dead tree branches.

You see, where we were living there were no dead tree branches around at all we had to go search for them. Sometimes I would wondered into the jungle with other adults and sometimes by myself once I had already been there once or twice. The scariest part to me was the possibility of being attacked by a large animal, like a tiger, bear, wild boar or snake.

I was so fearful of these animals attacking me, but the fear became less intense as I grew more and more hungry. Anyway, once I gathered some of the dead tree branches, I would try to find the vine and cut them off the trees with the machete I carried with me for that purpose. The machete was a great tool to have with me while searching for dead tree branches.

I would then lay down the long string of vine on each side,

left and right and then lay the bunch of dead tree branches on the vine and tied them up with it. I would do the same on the other side with the vine, and then I would cut up another long piece of tree branch about five feet long and hook it onto each end of the bunch that I tied with the vine, carrying it home on my shoulder.

I would repeat this process every day. Some days I would find extra dead tree branches, and some days I would find less. I got lost a few times on my way home because I wanted to stay longer and gather more tree branches.

One time I got lost on my way back home. There was no river to cross on my way to get the tree branches, but as I was on my way back home, I suddenly ran into a river. That was when I knew I was lost and had to find another way back home before it got dark. There was nobody around, and I had two big bunches of tied up dead tree branches with me.

I was staring at a river, and I wondered if crossing it would lead me home the short way. I did not have much time left before darkness set, and I knew that if I started to go back the other way without crossing the river, the sun would set, and I would be in deep trouble. I sat down and thought for a few minutes whether I should cross the river.

I sensed that crossing the river would lead me home the short way. I just had that feeling, plus I did not want to go back the other way; it would be too long, and I would probably get more lost and never find a way back home. So I made a decision to cross the river by myself and take a chance because I was scared and wanted to get home.

What scared me even more was that I did not know how to swim at that time, and I had to find a way to get to the other side of the river before the sun set. I set aside my fear and came up with the idea that if I could tie the two bunches of dead tree branches together, it may be able to float on the river, and I could hang onto it to get across. At least I knew then that logs and dead tree branches if tied together could float on water.

I had to make sure that I tied the two bunches of tree branches together tightly, so they would not break loose. With that done, I dropped the tree branches on the shallow part of the river to make sure that it would float before going on with it.

Much to my surprise, it did float, I guess because the branches were so dried out. I quickly pushed it out further on to the deeper part of the river and hung onto the tree branches with my life. While floating and holding onto the tree branches, I continued to kick my feet under water to gain momentum, hoping that I would not sink.

As I got closer to the other side of the river, I noticed that the tree branches had become loose, and I began to panic because I couldn't swim. With nothing left to hold on to, I said to myself, "I'm going to drown and die if I don't kick my feet harder under water and start to swim real hard, even though I didn't know how to swim."

Fighting as hard as I could to keep my head above water and knowing that if I didn't I would not make it to see my family again, I pushed and kicked very hard with both of my hands and feet. I made to the other side, and my foot was still kicking at the bottom of the shallow part of the river, and that was when I realized I made it across. I prayed hard for god to help me cross the river safely, and it worked.

Soaked in water and very tired, I thanked god again for saving me. Even though I lost all of the tree branches I had spent so many hours gathering, I was glad to have crossed the river.

My sense of direction was correct, as I found my way back home that evening; it turned out to be the short way. From that day on, I used the same route home, crossing the river without losing those valuable, much needed, tree branches. I felt like I was becoming a man because of the things that I had to do and my actions. I learned at a very young age to improvise and stay mentally strong and focus through hard times and believe that there is more than one way to do things. I also learned to swim by myself the hard way, the way I wish no one should have to go through by themselves.

I've gained survival skills and learned to trust my instincts when it comes to life and death and crucial situations. That's a lot for a kid to learn at a young age, but I had no one to teach me these things; self-teaching was the only choice for me to survive. My mother would always worry about me when I left to gather dried tree branches, especially after I told her about the day that I got lost by myself and had to learn how to swim across the river to get back home.

From then on I would always bring home lots of tree branches for my mother. Sometimes my mother would go to the river and gather lots of clams to cook for us, and we would have plenty to eat, and there would be much left over for the next day too. This was a good place the Khmer Rouge had put us in.

I learned very quickly how to search for dried tree branches in different areas. Sometimes you have to go deeper into the jungle in order to find the dead trees, but that's where I found most of them. I would get scared sometimes for my own safety if I went too deep into the jungle, but it didn't matter to me much; I just did it.

I think we were surviving better than most people because we knew how to search for food in different areas and we always planned ahead the next step we should take to survive.

Another way for us to continue searching for extra food was to go down to the river and dig for clams under water, and there were lots of them as I remember. Sometimes I would go with my mother to gather clams. Most people did not know that there were clams in the river at all. That was an advantage to us, and it sounds bad now, but we kept it to ourselves.

We would bring a bucket with us and fill it up with clams every time we went down to the river. After a while, my mother and I were pretty good at clam digging.

Leaving the bucket on the dry land, we would go under water and feel the muddy part on the bottom where all the clams were. We used our hands to pick these clams then wrap them in the waist part of our stretch pants until we got lots of them wrapped up around our waist. Then we would dump them into the bucket on dry land. We would repeat the procedure until we filled the bucket with clams. Some days it would take a long time to fill the bucket because there weren't many clams on the river, and we had to search a wider area, but by that time I already knew how to swim a little bit, so I really enjoy doing that. . The clams tasted great after they were cooked, and we had lots of them for ourselves. I'm not sure how we came to know of the clams on the river, but I was just glad we did. I owe it to my mother for all the things she was able to help us with.

We all wondered why and how my mother would have so much extra food when no one else could get any at all, at least not as much as she had.

It was a mystery to us until one day she told us an interesting story. While working on the pepper field, my mother met this older man who was the one that took care of the pepper farm. Fortunately that man was not one of the Khmer Rouge; he was one of us, and he was a very nice person as my mother had explained to us.

He knew of different secret places to get food, I guess because he had been a farmer all of his life. Anyhow, each day he would go out and pack a bag full of potatoes, taro, sugar cane, and red and green peppers for my mother to take home at the end of the day. My mother would be so happy and thankful that this man would do this for her. He would even tell her about some of the secret places where she could go search for the foods that he had given her.

She had never met anyone like this man since we were forced to live in this area. After a while this man opened up to my mother and told her that he had loved my mother since the first day he met her and now he wanted to marry her. My mother was shocked.

At that time, my mother wasn't sure whether he was Khmer Rouge or one of us. She was scared that he wanted to marry her, but one thing she knew for sure was that she did not want to marry anybody at all. All she wanted to do was meet a good person and find extra food for her family. So my mother had to come up with something fast that would not hurt his feelings, since he had done so much for her. That man gave my mother plenty of food.

My mother is a genius when it comes to finding the right words and things to say to someone in order to get out of trouble. She came up with an idea and told this man that she would not be able to marry him because she had a heart condition and sometimes would have seizures since her husband's death and time probably would not heal her. My mother explained that she lost her mom and brother too in the same year. She also told him that he was a great man with a big heart and she appreciated so much what he has done for her and wanted to be his friend.

He agreed and felt even sorrier for my mother that all these things had happened to her and her family. My mother later found out that he was one of us and definitely not Khmer Rouge, but she still did not want to marry anyone.

Taking care of her family was her priority, and she never let us down since my father, grandmother and uncle died.

My mother continued to receive extra food from this man even after she told him that she couldn't marry him. That was how nice and generous of a man he was to my mother. The extra food really helped us out a lot.

Even though we had some extra food, it still wasn't enough for everyone to be satisfied. We were all in need of essential vitamins for normal health; our bodies sometimes became weak and often swollen due to this problem. We started eating those red and green peppers. They were very spicy, but we thought eating them would help our immune systems. After a while, the swelling slowly went away. The peppers were like a medicine.

We continued eating those peppers everyday as much as we could handle, even though they were hot as hell. We got used to eating them pretty quickly and soon built a certain level of tolerance for the heat.

I got used to it because it was life or death. I guess the Khmer

Rouge, as evil as they were, had given us a break by letting us stay in this part of the country where there was at least some extra food. Also, having us live by the river was a big relief, as we could survive for much longer because we had water.

Chapter 7

I remembered one horrifying thing while we lived in this part of the countryside. The Khmer Rouge continued to watch over us, making sure we were not doing anything they didn't want us to do. One of the leaders of the Khmer Rouge in this area was named Hai, at least it was pronounced that way. This man had killed many innocent Cambodians, including women, children and, occasionally, pregnant women with children still in their wombs.

He hated people who looked or sounded like they were educated, clean, rich, or well groomed. Sometimes he would identify these people and take them out to torture them first and then have them killed. Sometimes he would take a torturing device to take their finger nails out one by one to have them suffer, then beat their heads with a hammer or a piece of stick until they died.

Sometimes he would tie them up and beat them and stab them with the rifle and then carve out their eyeballs to finish them off.

After that, he would sometimes cut them up, take their hearts out, cook them and eat them. This was beyond cruelty, but it was a reality.

There were many witnesses to these things. Some of the victims did not have a chance to even try to escape before being captured and executed.

Some said that they had seen him kill people and cook their hearts in a frying pan just like it was nothing to him. The people who saw this happen and were fortunate enough to escape told some of us that when they saw him cook the human hearts it was not like cooking regular meat. The human hearts were big, and when he cooked them in a frying pan they would jump up and down like they were going to explode.

It would also take much longer to cook the human heart because it was so big. Sometimes, we were told, he would eat the heart before it was completely cooked.

The people that witness this cruel ordeal would often have nightmares about this evil man, and they were afraid living there.

When we heard about this, we did not believe it at all until more people came forward and told us the same story. After we all heard about this, everything changed; we thought that we might be a little safer in this place, but we were wrong. All the torturing and killings has been done here quietly.

We were so horrified of this situation that we could not trust whether any one was a Khmer Rouge spy, gathering information in order to destroy us.

My family and I would often get nightmares, knowing all of

this torturing and killing of innocent people was happening so close to where we were. "We were living in a nightmare".

Several times during the daytime I did not feel well and didn't want to go to work. Maybe I was so scared of what had happened I wanted to just stay home and hide from the Khmer Rouge. That didn't work out very well for me.

The Khmer Rouge came looking for me at the place where we stayed. They would scream and yell again, "Where is Bunthong?" At the time, my mother had not left for work yet, and I would run to the corner of the room and try to hide from them, but it didn't take them long to find me. I cannot explain the fear I had when they found me at home.

I was afraid that they would take me away from my family or maybe kill me the way that those other people had been killed. My mother tried to protect me and told the Khmer Rouge that I was sick and could not work that day and to please give me a break; but no matter what my mother said, they took me away anyway.

I thought they were going to kill me, but they only wanted me to go to work. They dragged me around and dropped me off at the wheat field. My mother also thought that I might be killed that day. I got to come back home that evening, and my mother was so happy to see me. She thought she had lost me.

When you are a kid, and you see and hear all of these horrible things that are happening around you, you get scared and started tripping out. That was true in my case. My mind was messing with me all the time. Even when they didn't want to kill me, I thought that they did.

My mother and the people around thought the same thing. That was how messed up we all were whenever we saw these people come by and yell at us and order us to go somewhere else. In our minds we told ourselves that they were going to torture and kill us.

Everything changed now that we knew about the killings; we needed to find a way to escape this place. No matter how many ways we thought of to escape, it wasn't going to happen because the Khmer Rouge were everywhere, armed with their guns, rifles and machetes. We would have all kinds of ideas and plans of what to do next, but we could not carry them out because we were more scared of being caught.

My mother had a plan to escape at night, or when it got real late or even during the daytime when everyone was at work and the Khmer Rouge took their break, but we didn't do it because no one would know where to go. First of all, we did not know our way around the countryside or how to even go from this area. We were scared out of our minds about being caught by the Khmer Rouge.

If we all decided to escaped and ever got caught by the Khmer Rouge, we would all be dead for sure and we were not willing yet to take that risk.

So escape was only a dream at that time. We hung onto each other as close as we all could and tried very hard to survive while living each day in fear, under control of the Red Cambodians. One thing that helped us along the way was that we had hopes and faith that one day something good would happen because we were good people and good human beings. That was the only thing that got us through each day.

Chapter 8

Later on in 1976, I was taken away by the Khmer Rouge and separated from my mother, sister and brother. All they told my mother was they were going to take her son to stay and work in different part of the country with other boys, and he would not be back anytime soon.

That devastated my mother; the only productive son she had at the time helping her gather food and goods would be separated from her. I was also devastated.

Not knowing what would happen to me next made my mother feel incredibly sad to say the least. There was nothing my mother could have said or do to prevent this from happening; the Khmer Rouge decided that I would be living somewhere else with a group of other young kids. My sister was forcibly separated from my mother and sent to different part of the country to work with other young teens. So my mother was left with my young brother who was at the time only four years old and was too young to work somewhere else. He was ordered by the Khmer Rouge to stay with mom.

That was the only reason they didn't take him away from my mother. I'm not sure how my sister felt; I was the first to go. My sister was separated from my mother right after I was taken away.

When I was taken from my family, I felt lonely and scared. All I knew was that I would never see my mother, sister and brother again. You just don't do that to a kid when he has already have lost his grandmother, father and uncle and has seen and heard of all the horrible torturing and killings. To me at the time it felt like the end of the world.

I felt, lost and confused and scared for my life all over again. I'm sure that my sister felt the same way when she was separated from my mother and brother. They would not tell my mother where they took me; all they told her was he would be with a group of young kids working in different part of the country.

I was forced to live in this shelter made out of bamboo along with other kids around my age. The roof was made of coconut tree leaves bound together, like the one my family was living under. The bed was also made of bamboo tied together in a row with some vines, and there were big gaps left in between each stalk. It was the hardest and most uncomfortable bed I have ever slept on. Really it wasn't a bed, just some bamboo tied together in a row sitting on a two by four lift up by small foundations.

My bed was the least of my problems. I missed my family, and there were not much food. I was scared and lonely even though I was with other kids. Nothing replaces your family.

They only fed us one small bowl of soup rice, twice a day.

I would be lucky if they gave me some salt to go with the soup rice. The amount of food they gave me was not nearly enough to make me feel full or satisfy in any way. There must have been something about the soup rice that they loved to make for us because that's all they fed us day after day. The Khmer Rouge loved to see us starve. We would again be starving hungry everyday; we needed much more than a small bowl of soup rice.

The Khmer Rouge ordered me to go work in the field, stacking hay and planting rice along with other young kids my age. In the morning they would have us planting wheat and by afternoon they would have us stacking hay until evening time. The weather was always hot and by midday the temperature would reach around 90 to 100 degree with high humidity. It was horrible!

The hot weather and high humidity could kill someone very easily, especially kids working in the field. The Khmer Rouge forced it upon us and we had to follow their orders; there were no other options whatsoever.

The more we suffered the more they enjoyed it.

They separated me from my family and forced me to live with other kids and perform the work of an adult. To me the work that they made us do was overwhelming and torturing, especially when there were not enough food to eat each day and we were all starving. They did not provide adequate water for us, even during the hottest day at work when the temperature would reach around 100 plus degrees.

The Khmer Rouge would torture us that way to see how many could survive under these harsh conditions. It was like a cruel game they were playing with everyone, and, by the look in their eyes, they enjoyed it. They not only abused us physically but also mentally. They would often call us stupid and worthless while we were working on the wheat fields. We all worked very hard and did not deserve these harsh words on top of the physical labor they brought upon us.

Each day after we all got back to the shelter, a bowl of soup rice was given to each one of us kids along with some salt. I know I'm repeating things, but it was the truth. I saw kids my age get sick from starvation and some died from it. Some died next to me during the night and had to be removed and disposed of the next morning without notifying their parents. That was horrifying to me!

I told myself that I had to do something about this situation or I would die of starvation too. I had to find a way to search for extra food for myself in order to survive this ordeal. So each day, when I was on my way to and from work on the wheat field, I would take my time looking around the area to see if there was anything edible that I could come back for later.

If I saw any food along the way, you bet I found a way to get it no matter what it took. If I had to I would come back at night to get it; that was how determined I was. This was life or death!

As I scanned around the area, I noticed there were some cornfields and some sugar cane fields not too far from where we were staying. I also saw some taro popping from the ground near the corn fields; that meant there was taro under the ground that I could dig up later and eat, but I would have to come back later at night. That was my plan.

The Khmer Rouge would see me if I did it during the day, plus there were other kids around, and that would not be good. I wouldn't tell anybody that I saw this food because I didn't want any other kids to know about it. It wasn't that I didn't want them to have any, but I was more afraid that they would go and tell some other kids and sooner or later the Khmer Rouge would find out and I would be in trouble or even be killed.

Not that I was a bad person or kid, I just didn't want to cause a commotion because I knew it would be bad. That was why I didn't want anybody else to know about this secret. I learned the secret of searching for taro that most kids did not know about. Here's how it worked: When you see a bump on the ground all you have to do is remove the dirt and most of the time there would be taro under ground, that's how it grew. I learned that trick while I was with my family living in a different area of the country.

I thought out a plan that when it got dark and became night time and all of the kids have gone to sleep and the Khmer Rouge were taking their breaks from guarding the area, I would set out to search for the food that I saw earlier.

I was not afraid of anything because starvation took over my body and I was on a mission to find food. I no longer thought about the consequences I would face if the Khmer rouge caught me. I was oblivious.

That was how desperate I was and I told my self I was not going to die of starvation like these other kids if I could help it. That was how mentally strong I was as a kid, and I wanted to live to see my family again someday. When all the kids were sleeping I would take off by myself in the dark, the only light that I saw was the light from the shining moon as I searched my way around the area for food. I tried to focus on remembering where I had seen those things.

I remember looking at the ground patiently searching for the taros that I saw earlier in the day. I finally ran into a couple of bumps on the ground and then some more bumps and that's where all of the taro was planted and grew. I was so happy and started digging with my hands and pulled out a couple of long taro roots about 12 inches long, and that was all I wanted and needed at the time.

I moved on to the sugar cane fields nearby, knowing that I could always come back to the taro area again tomorrow. I knew exactly where the sugar cane fields were because they were tall and looked different from the cornfields. I headed there after I got the taros in the small bag. When I got to the sugar cane fields, I broke a couple of branches off and just started sucking the juices off those two branches because I was so thirsty and hungry. The sugar canes were sweet and tasted incredible to me and I couldn't believe I found the fields even at night. I thought to my self I was good!

Once I was done I went back to the shelter with the two pieces of taro and I planned to cook them in the open fire that the Khmer Rouge had build during the evening to cook soup rice for us. The fire was still burning in some area and there was nobody around, so I started to insert the two pieces of taro into the fire to attempt to cook them. I planned all these things out while receiving the bowl of rice earlier in the evening.

I knew that the fire would still be burning until late at night because it was a big fire and big fire lasts much longer.

Before I know it, the taro was completely cooked. I had a couple of big taro roots to eat and they tasted so incredibly good. I was actually full for the first time ever since I arrived there. After I was finished with the taros, I felt very satisfied and went back to bed without anyone noticing me.

I tried to sleep with a full stomach, but I couldn't do it because my stomach was too full and I had to wait a while. I felt happy at the same time because I was actually full for once. All I thought was that I could not believe I found extra food for myself, cooked it, ate it and did not get caught. It was the most incredible feeling for a kid to accomplish, and I thought to myself I'm going to do it again tomorrow. No one will stop me now, and next time I will go for the cornfields too.

Knowing that I could do this again the next day I was

very excited. When I went to work on the wheat fields, I felt stronger and had much more energy than the other kids. I felt bad that the other kids did not know what I knew then; but what could I do? I felt happy even though I was overworked because I knew when night time came around I would be full again and that was what drove me to not let work bother me too much during the day.

So during the next night I went out and did the same thing again, but this time I took corn back instead of taro. I switched every night between the two for a while. I could not believe that I got away with this every night. Sometimes my stomach would be so full, but I was still able to sleep at night because I got used to it. When I had to go to pee at night I was so afraid to get up because I had a guilty conscience, and I was afraid the Khmer Rouge might catch me. So I came up with another idea.

What I did when I had to pee at night was turn around and just pull my pants down and stick my penis through between the bamboo bed and pee through it slowly so no one would hear me. This turned out to be a great idea because no one even noticed anything throughout the night. Sometimes it would rain, and the rain would wash the pees away under the bamboo bed.

I continued to do this for a long time because I was surviving big time and it felt so good to be full every night. I also felt a sense of accomplishment because I was brave enough to do this by myself and no one helped me.

I knew that I didn't want to starve to death. It was not the way I wanted to die. I told my self time and time again that I would do whatever it took to find extra food even if it meant stealing from the Khmer Rouge or any body else. I would not die from starvation!

Even if I was to get caught by the Khmer Rouge or someone else and ultimately pay the price for it, I was willing to sacrifice. I often wondered also why the other kids did not try to do what I did to help them stay alive, because to me it was worth it. Maybe they were scared of being caught or maybe they just didn't know where to look. Anyway, some of them starved to death, and to me that was not an option. I was willing to risk getting caught and possibly killed. I guess what most people do not understand is when you get to a point where you are so hungry you will do unimaginable things. I was in that situation and had to do what was necessary.

Chapter 9

While I was surviving in this area, my sister was sent to a place far away from me and from my mother and brother. She was sent to work with some fishermen out on the boat. Her job was to clean all the fish that they caught for the Khmer Rouge leaders. I think my sister kind of got lucky when they sent her to work on the river because the work was light and there would always be fish to eat. My sister had told me that she was lucky.

They would send her out on the boat everyday with men who were forced by The Red Cambodians to go out on the boat and net fish for them. They often had to go far out on the river to catch fish. Some of these men were very nice people who were just like any of us trying to survive each day while working for the Khmer Rouge.

They didn't let my sister do any of the fishing or netting because she couldn't swim. Her job was to just stay on the boat while these guys took care of netting and fishing. Once they gathered enough fish on the boat, my sister's job was to gut them out and clean them up for the leaders.

Some of the guys would have left over fish and they often gave them to my sister. They gave her enough to eat where she was also surviving. Even though she was brought to a place where there was food and the work was not overwhelming, the danger was always there because my sister could not swim and she was forced to go out on the boat in a deep river with no life jacket or anything like that. These Red Cambodians didn't care whether my sister could swim or not; all they wanted her and the other men to do was go out on the river and do what they were told. If they complained about anything in regards to work or anything else they might be the next ones to die without warning. Their lives were pretty much meaningless to the Khmer Rouge.

My sister told me a story; One day she was cleaning and gutting the fish on the boat and one jumped out. She tried to grab it before it went into the water, but she leaned over too far and fell in. The guys in the front of the boat did not see or hear my sister fall from the boat, so basically she was drowning there for a short time. She tried to kick and fight to stay afloat, but she was slowly going down.

As she was going down, a man turned around and saw my sister and ran by to pull her from the river. My sister thought that she was going to drown and die in the river; it was the scariest thing she had experienced. Someone was looking out for her that fateful day on the river.

My sister also told me that while she was working on the river she got really sick. She had some kind of a virus that really took a toll on her body. For weeks she suffered from diarrhea, fever, and bouts of vomiting. She lost so much weight that she was almost just skin and bones, much like my uncle was before he died. She thought she was going to die also because mom and other family members weren't around to take care of her.

My mother did not know where they had taken my sister. The Khmer Rouge never told us where she was or where they took her. All they said to mom was they were taking her away to have her work in a different area of the country. My mother must have been so terrified! Nothing the Khmer Rouge did made any sense to me or anybody.

It was much like what they did to me when they took me away from my mother. My sister was lucky that some of the men she worked with cared enough about her to help her out, providing her with some food and of course fish so that she could get better. For some miraculous reason my sister pulled out of that incredible sickness. Without doubt, it should have killed her.

She was very lucky; I guess it wasn't her time to go yet. Once she recovered from her sickness, she was forced to go back to work, but this time on the dock instead of on the river. For some strange reason the Khmer Rouge changed their minds about her work assignment. Maybe the men that she worked with said something to the Khmer Rouge to persuade them to change their minds about having my sister work on the dock instead, especially after what had happened to her. Whatever it was, she was very thankful that she did not have to go back out on the river again. Being on the river and not knowing how to swim was a nightmare to her.

I was still doing ok at the village where I was at and still trying hard to survive the best I could. I had mastered different routes to get to the place with the extra food, so I wouldn't get caught. At least I prayed I wouldn't get caught.

I knew that if I kept going at the same time and in the same direction, one day someone would find out and I would get caught. I was constantly thinking of a different route, and it always seemed to work.

Until one night I had to go poop while in the cornfield, and that was when trouble arose. I went away from the area where I went to poop. I went toward the end of the cornfield, which I thought was a great idea because I didn't want to just poop right where I was. I thought I might step on my own poop while moving around the area.

I wanted to make sure that I didn't poop in the middle of the cornfield because I would be back the next night, and I could step on it. If I were to step on my own poop, everyone would know it the next day for sure.

The reason that I planned to go poop at the end of the cornfield is that I would remember where I pooped and I could avoid stepping on it later. There would be evidence if I was to accidentally step on my own poop, and there would be no way to wipe the poop off completely at night, and it would stink and someone would have a suspicion about me. So now you know why I had to go to the end of the cornfield to poop. Almost everything I did I had to plan ahead.

After I was done pooping I got up and picked up the corn that I had picked earlier and rolled it back into my stretch pants. As I turned around to walk back, there were a few of the Khmer Rouge pointing their rifles at me and ordering me to walk with them. I was shocked at that moment the Khmer rouge caught me. I heard no footstep while I was pooping and had no idea that they were close by, maybe because I was concentrating so much of what I had to do and didn't hear them coming.

They were asking me what I was doing there and how I knew of this place where the cornfields are? My answers as I was trying to save myself was, "I came here to poop and I got lost and could not find my way back to where I came from." They looked at me and yelled at me in a loud voice, "Then why did you have some corn with you?" I told them I was hungry and could not help but pick some when I saw them.

I told them, "I'm hungry and desperate; please forgive me for what I did; it was a mistake." I begged them to let me go and I would try to find my way back to the place I came from. I even try to cry, but the tears never came out from my eyes because I had been through enough hard times that it didn't matter any more. They never let me go no matter what I said to them.

So the Khmer Rouge brought me to this place in the middle of nowhere in the jungle. This is the place where they all went together when they captured people that they didn't like and decided whether to kill them or not. Most of the time the odds are against you if these people captured you. You would be tortured and then killed.

By the time they brought me to this place, it was already morning and the sun came up. I could see there were a few men being dragged and beaten with a baseball bat-like piece of wood and rifle. The Khmer Rouge guys screamed and yelled, and most of the words that came out of their mouths were about the killing and suffering that these men will have to face.

At this time I didn't know why these men were tied up and being beaten so badly by the Khmer Rouge; all I knew was that they, like me, were going to die. There was no question that I was in big trouble and there was no way out of it. I prayed so hard and I wanted someone to feel sorry for me so I could stay alive to see my family again.

They proceed to tie me up against a small tree with some vines and started to ask me more questions. They asked me things like: Do you have a mother and father? Who are they? What do they do? Where are they now? All of these questions made me think that if I answered the way they wanted me to or if I had told them the truth, they would hunt my mother and family down and kill them all. So I had to think of a lie to tell them, and I had to do it quickly because they were pressuring me to answer. Guns were pointed at me as questions were directed at me.

I told the Khmer Rouge that I was an orphan and did not have a living mother or father. I told them I lived with a bunch of other kids around my age in a village not too far from where they found me. I told them that I was hungry and needed food in order to survive. I told them that the only reason why I picked the corn. I continued to beg them to let me go so I could be back with the other kids.

I wanted so badly for them to believe all of my answers. I wanted them to know that I was sincere, even though I wasn't. I wanted them to feel very sorry for me so that they would let me go back to the place that I came from. "At least," I thought to my self, "don't kill me". I wasn't ready to die yet.

My answers didn't help me much, but they did not ask me anymore about my family. They stopped asking me questions and started beating me with some pieces of sticks, taking turn continuously until one side of my body became bruised and swollen. The pain was unbearable, but I had to take it.

After the first beating, they again proceed to ask me the same questions, hoping that my answers would be different, but I never gave in to their demand. My answers would always be the same because I did not want them to find out I had a family and that some of them were still alive. I knew if the Khmer Rouge found out I had a family, they would be in danger.

If I told them the truth they would definitely have hunted down my mother, sister and brother to torture or possibly kill them too. The beating and the pain were excruciating, and they did not stop the beating until I was almost passed out. When you get beat up so badly your body becomes numb to a point where you no longer feel much pain anymore and your brain just accepts it. That was what happened to me.

They continued to beat me down with some sticks whip me with vines until I was in and out of consciousness. I vaguely recall this, but all of a sudden the beating stopped. I didn't know why they stopped, but I was glad they did.

All the time that they beat on me and yelled at me I never cried; I told myself to think about my family and pray to god that they would not kill me. I had gotten to the point where beating was something I could accept as long as they didn't kill me.

After the beating stopped just as I was about to pass out, they gave me a cup of water and untied my hands from the tree. They picked me up and threw me into a small shed and gave me some soup rice to eat along with some fish. None of them said anything to me; they just gave me the food and walked off.

I was shocked that they actually gave me some soup rice and a fish to eat; I hadn't had soup rice in a long time let alone fish. They have always given us soup rice to eat before but never with fish. I ate the soup rice and the fried fish, and then I passed out.

When I woke up I saw several Khmer Rouge standing over me carrying guns and rifles. They asked if I spoke Cambodian?

I was so confused and scared I didn't know what to think. I told them that I was in a lot of pain and needed medicine. They all started laughing at me and told me that I was very lucky that they didn't kill me.

The last thing I remember they all said to me before letting me go was "get out of here and get out of here fast!" Despite the pain all over my body, I ran as fast as I could away from them. I could not believe that they let me go after all the beating they did to me. I never knew the real reason why they decided to let me go; maybe they really just felt sorry for me at that particular moment because I was so young and had told them that I was an orphan living with other kids. Those answers that I thought of may have saved my life then. I really don't know for sure.

After I was let go by the Khmer Rouge, I ran for a long time. I just wanted to get as far away from them as possible. I didn't know what else to do then except to keep on running. I managed to find my way back to the village where I was staying at with all the other kids.

By this time it was already in the evening, and no one was at the shelter where all the kids were suppose to be; I guess they were still at work but would be back anytime. So I cleaned myself up and got on the bamboo bed and just lay there waiting for the kids to come back from work so I could join them for dinner. I felt so sore all over my body from the beating, but I didn't tell anyone.

I also thought that if any of the kids or the Khmer Rouge

ask me where I was at, I would just tell them that I was sick and I went to look for a place to throw up and poop last night but got lost and took the wrong way back and finally found my way home this morning. I would also tell them that I was too sick and tired to go to work today. I was only about ten years old then, and that was the best answer I could think of.

I was hoping that no one would notice that I was gone the previous night or better yet I was praying that the Khmer Rouge in this village did not pay attention to where I disappeared.

I stole other kid's pants and shirt to wear while they were at work to cover up my bruised and swollen body. I was also lucky that my face did not have many bruises, just some scratches I gained while running through some bushes to get back to the shelter. Although my body hurt badly from the beating my face looked decent enough not to draw too much attention. The stolen pants and shirt covered the bruises well.

When all the kids came back from working on the field, I was still laying in bed pretending that I was really sick. I shook like a little animal that had just been born to make it look real to other kids. Only a few kids that slept close to me noticed that I was gone the night before. They asked me where I had been and what I had been doing the previous night?

"Where were you this morning?" I told them the story about getting lost while looking for a place to throw up and poop. Even though I knew that was not the most believable answer, it was good enough for the kids that noticed I was gone the night before. I was very fortunate that none of the Khmer Rouge noticed that I had been missing. To be honest I wouldn't have known what else to say to them if they had demanded answers. Again someone looked out for me and helped me in this situation; maybe it was luck, or maybe it was god. That evening I got the regular soup rice like everyone else, and I was glad to just be alive and able to sleep again along with the other kids.

The next morning, with pain all over my body, I went to work like everyone else, but I did not show it because if I did, everyone, including the Khmer Rouge, would know and certainly ask more questions. I did not want to deal with any more questions. The saddest part about this was that I would not be able to go out at night again to look for extra food while I was still living in this area because I was too afraid that I would get caught again.

I told myself over and over, "don't go out to do this again at night" just to be sure I wouldn't. I knew that if I did it again and got caught I would not be so lucky.

I still had hope that one day I would see my family again and that was what drove me to do some of the things that I did to keep myself alive. I never gave up like some of the other kids in the village. I convinced myself not to look for food at night until things changed. I knew then that things would always change as long as we lived under the Khmer Rouge control.

Chapter 10

After spending about six months living with other kids away from my mother, sister and brother, I was forced again to move to a different area of the country. I saw this change coming as I mentioned it before. I think the Khmer Rouge never wanted all of us to stay in one area for a long period of time. As we struggled with starvation and became familiar with one area, they forced us to move to another. I believe their idea was to have everyone suffer in one area of the country and when some had figured out how to survive there the Khmer Rouge forced them to move, assuming they survived.

It was like a game of death they were playing with our lives. Basically they used us like slaves and gave us very little food to see who could survive. They moved whoever survived to another place to start the nightmares all over again.

I had to move again along with some other kids from the previous village to another village where we were forced to live with other adults. There were only several kids at my age in this new village. It was a small village with nothing much around it but some trees and uneven ground. We all had to share a small hut. All the other adults stayed in other huts nearby in the village. We all followed the men to work each morning in the new wheat field far away from the village.

We would wake up early in the morning before the sunrise and ride the cow carriage with other adults to work. When we got there our job was to plant some more wheat on the empty fields as needed. Once all the wheat has been planted in one field we were expected to move on to another empty field and do it all over again. Sometimes some of us were ordered to go and stack some hay or remove dirt and mud from one area to another to form a walkway around the fields.

This type of work was just too hard and heavy for a kid to perform, but there was no way out of it. We pretty much performed the work of an adult. While helping the other adults plant rice on the new wheat fields, we came across many blood-sucking leeches of all sizes. I was petrified.

Sometimes I would plant the wheat without knowing that these leaches were all over my body until I got out of the field. The leeches would cling onto my skin like a piece of really sticky tape, and it was very hard to remove them as they buried their heads into my skin, sucking the living daylights out of my body. A lot of the time I just let the leeches continued to suck my blood for a period of time before I could come out of the water to get them off my skin.

There were so many leeches in the wheat field that sometimes I could see them swimming around the surface of the water if I looked closely. I couldn't help it but let them cling onto me and suck my blood because the minute that I tried to put my foot or hand or any part of my body in the water the leeches were all over me in almost an instant. The Khmer Rouge were constantly watching us from above the wheat field so we couldn't just get in the wheat field and get out immediately just because there were leeches on our bodies; we wouldn't get any work done and they would take us out and have us killed without any hesitation what so ever.

So everyone working on the field just let the leeches suck on them for a while until it started to hurt before coming out of the field to remove them. I would let the leeches have the best of me before I could come out of the water to get them off. The big leeches they called the buffalo leeches didn't scare me at all because I could feel them once they were on me.

The little leeches were what really made me have nightmares because I could not tell whether they were on me or not; I couldn't feel them a lot of the time when they were on me. When we bent down to plant the wheat on the field, the water level came up to about knee high for an adult, but for me and other kids, the water level came up to about my waist, and that was a big problems.

Sometimes the leaches would get all the way up my crotch and onto the penis area and cling on. There were several times where I found those tiny leeches on my penis and I couldn't feel they were on me because I was busy concentrating on planting wheat. I got out of the water to take some of the other leeches out and looked inside my pants and there they were on my penis. It scared the living daylights out of me as soon as I saw those creepy little leeches on my penis. It took me forever to remove them. Once the leeches are on your skin, they stick like glue. The tiny leeches were hard to get a hold of with your fingers, plus it was slippery too.

I eventually figured out a way to keep those leeches off of me. I would tie the bottom of my pants on both sides with two strings, one on each side, to prevent them from coming into contact with my legs. For my arms, I would tie both sides of my long sleeve shirt at the wrist area with strings. It was a brilliant idea!

That worked like magic, and I thought I came up with a very smart idea for a kid. I shared that idea with other kids and adults that worked in the same field. No leeches ever slipped through those tight strings.

Although I could not prevent the leeches from clinging onto my hands, I didn't mind. As long as they didn't get onto my body, I was happy. It was bad enough being overworked on the fields like an animal, but to also have my life being sucked out by these leeches from hell was another thing. I wasn't going to let it happen for long.

I was so exhausted on my way back from work each day. I would feel so weak that I could have passed out anytime. In this part of the country food was again scarce. We had to go out and hunt for ourselves anything that was available. Usually it would be frogs and crabs and sometimes fish.

We all had accepted what the Khmer Rouge has given us. It was getting old and repetitious, just a bowl of soup rice for lunch and again for dinner. It was unimaginable and heartless. Nothing tasted good, and we were all losing weight very quickly. Some of us were dying slowly.

I recall a frightening experience on my way back from work where I saw several dead kids. Many flies gathered around their mouths; it was horrible. From the look of it, they must have been dead for a while. The swelling of their body was a good indication, plus the smell was so bad.

I also saw some older adults die around the village. Some had died from starvation and some from apparent gunshot wounds to their heads. The dead people were just left on the field and in the middle of the road. Sometimes we would discover dead people on the roadside on our way back from work. Some were left under the mango tree rotting away. I often thought to myself "please let it be a nightmare so I can wake up soon and all of this will go away. Unfortunately it wasn't.

The gruesome discovery shocked me and left me with permanent emotional scars. For god's sake, I was only a kid. I didn't have a choice not to see those things happen as they were; it was very sad and unfortunate. The suffering that people endured and the killings that the Khmer Rouge did made no sense to me. The bad thing was they enjoyed killing innocent people. It put a smile on their faces as we could see when they talked.

They really enjoyed every aspect of torturing and killing people. There were a lot of dead people scattered everywhere around the fields and the roadside. There were dead people left under mango trees, especially the big mango trees. There must be something about the mango trees that cause the Khmer Rouge to leave the people they have killed under them. There must be some sort of belief. Sometimes they even hanged people on the mango trees.

I used to see dead people hung on mango trees on my way back from work. Sometimes I would ignore it and pretend that it wasn't there.

We all had to ride to and from work each day in some cow carriages. There must have been at least twelve people per carriage. There was barely any room for us to sit in the carriage. Sometimes I had to sit in the little space and hang on to the side of the carriage so I wouldn't fall off. This was the only transportation we had.

On several occasions strange things happened to us on our way back from working on the field. One evening we all rode the cow carriage back from work very late. It was already dark by the time we left the field and it would take us at least half an hour to get back on the carriage.

We were the only carriage that had to stay that late that evening. All the other carriages had left earlier. Anyway, as soon as we got to the area where all the mango trees were and where some of people had been killed and left to rot out, the two big cows that were carrying our carriage all of a sudden just stopped moving. The cows just froze right in front of us and then started jumping up and down, moving backward, and making like they had seen a ghost or something. None of us had any idea what the heck the cows were doing because they never did that before; they were spooked by something very strange. We all looked at each other in horror and thought this was not right.

The cows continue to jump up and down and move backward and then forward for several minutes while we all were on the carriage trying to figure out why they did this weird thing and we were scared also. All of a sudden I heard a creepy voice of a baby crying from the mango tree. I was scared and started to ask the adults if they had heard the voice of a baby crying on the tree? It was very scary and creepy.

The adults told me that they had heard the same thing. We all looked at each other again and figured that there were no babies that we could see up on the tree but we heard a baby's voice crying like it was being tortured; it was the scariest sound that I could ever imagine. This was the place where all the killings had happened and the bodies dumped earlier and were rotting away.

A minute or so has gone by and the cows continued their strange behavior; we were all frightened by this sound of a baby crying without seeing it. It could only be one thing: a ghost of a baby or babies. There was definitely a child ghost or ghosts around the area and obviously the cows had seen the ghost and started to freak out in front of us in the dark. When we figured this out, we all just sat quietly in our carriage and started to pray that it would stop so we could get home.

A few minutes later the cows finally stopped jumping and moving backward and settled down to a calm and steady position again. Without speaking to one another, we waited for the cows until they were ready to move forward again.

We all got back to the village safely that night and got our share of the soup rice and went to sleep. I had nightmares of ghosts and other witches all night long and could not sleep well. The next morning we all got on the same carriage and went to work again. We talked about what had happened the night before. Several other kids and adults told me they were having the same nightmares.

From this point on we hoped that we didn't have to work late into the night again. We truly believed the cows that pulled our carriage had seen ghosts too. There were no other explanations why they would behave the way they did. I didn't believe in ghosts before this incident.

Many people told me ghost stories before, and I would listen but never believe any of it. Old people told me they have seen ghosts around the village. I ignored what they had told me completely; however, since that incident with the cows, I now believe in ghosts. There had to be a reason why the cows would freak out in the middle of the road with nothing in front of it that we could see. We all heard haunting baby's voices crying out of the mango tree, but there were no babies around. There were ghosts around that caused all this commotion, and it terrified all of us that night.

That was the scariest night for me and the other people riding on the carriage. The reason that we knew what we heard was the haunting voices of baby ghosts crying out were that we had seen dead babies under the mango tree before.

From this point on I begged the men to put me in the middle of the carriage as we rode it to and from work each day. Since I was the youngest in the group at the time, they were willing to do that for me. A few weeks later we heard a similar story about the other cow carriages, but instead of the haunting voices of the baby ghosts, they heard haunting voices of a mother echoing on the tree at night.

The cows that pulled their carriages had done the same thing as our cows did. Each hair on the back of my neck is standing up right now as I am telling you this true story. Even though it sounds unbelievable, it was true. Sometimes the Khmer Rouge would switch people from different carriages and demand that some stay late into the night to finish work on the fields.

The minute that I heard they were going to switch people to different carriages I was scared out of my mind that I might get rotated to a different carriage that had to stay late. If that were to happen I would be dealing with a scary situation with the ghosts again. I was petrified. Unfortunately, one of the Khmer rouge had rotated me to a different carriage that had to stay late. I did not want to go through that experience again with the ghosts again.

Once the Khmer Rouge had designated me to stay late, I had to move myself over to a different carriage that was going to go home early before dark. I had to sneak behind the Khmer Rouge in order to do this. There were more than a few carriages that took all of us to and from work and thank god that the Khmer Rouge did not notice at all that I was switching carriages. I was also fortunate that I was a small kid then and was able to barely fit myself onto the other carriage, hanging on for a ride back home after work.

No one ever mentioned anything about the ghosts we had seen and heard to the Khmer Rouge. We all knew we had to keep it to ourselves. We knew they wouldn't care to hear about it, plus if we would have said anything at all to them, they probably wouldn't have liked it, and we would all be in jeopardy. We only talked about this among ourselves when they were not around to hear.

Chapter 11

By this time I really had missed my family very much and due to the misery of the place and the work that I had to endure. I was haunted by nightmares almost every night about different things that I went through while I was at that village. I didn't have enough food to eat each day, I went through serious weight lost but yet my body looks like it was swollen up especially around the stomach area due to lacks of nutrition and vitamins.

Each day I was wishing I had more food to eat or that I could find a place somewhere where I could at least discover extra food, but it wasn't happening because this place had no food to offer. The place was dry and everything had died out; even water was hard to find, and we got water only through a well, and sometimes the well was also dried up. It was a horrible situation I was in.

Sometimes I would save the small baby crabs that I found on the field so I could eat when I got back to the village. I was so desperate for food that anything would do. Those baby crabs were the only extra food I could depend on, and it wasn't much.

I don't remember how long I had to live in this horrible

village. I call it the village of death. Months passed, and I became sick to the point where I could no longer go to work. I had diarrhea and stomach infections. At some point I felt like I was going to die without seeing my family again. I could not take much food in because it would come right back out. We didn't have much food to eat in this village anyway.

I was so terribly sick that nothing I ate would stay in. I was in big trouble! I couldn't eat much of anything. I had to beg the Khmer Rouge to help me. They decided to take me away from the village and have me stay in a so-called "hospital" with other very sick kids.

The hospital they took me to was big and dark. I could also see that there were other very sick adults around, but the place contained more kids than adults. I guess they decided to mix everyone together for some reason. Maybe there were no other places for the adults to go.

I felt so sad and thought to myself "this probably will be the place where I am going to die". I saw my grandmother and uncle die in similar places.

I remember a few people came to check up on me through out the day to see how I was doing. I realized then that it might be a real hospital after all. Maybe it was just a dream or hallucination.

While I was here, they gave me soup rice again, but this time around the soup rice was thicker, and the bowl was bigger, I could see the difference. They also gave us salty eggs to go with the thick soup rice instead of salt. That was something new I never had before. I was sick, and my stomach was swollen up. So were parts of my ankles and legs; but when I saw the hot thick soup rice with salty eggs, I wanted to eat it so badly. They never gave me any salty eggs to go with any of my food before, only salt and that was it with watery soup rice.

My eyes got bigger, and I started to chow down on the thick hot soup rice with salty eggs. I ate my fill and started to throw half of it back out. At least I had half of it in my stomach to hold me down for a while. I never wanted to die, and that was my way of fighting even though I was sick and couldn't take any food at the time.

I forced myself to eat and was eating more than I should because I didn't want to die, and if I happened to die, I wanted to die eating as much as I could.

Days went by, and I thought I was getting better because my swollen stomach was coming down a little bit, and I started to feel a little bit better too. I felt a sense of relief knowing that I didn't have to go to work out on the wheat fields while I was in this place. That gave me hope that as long as I was given a chance to stay here I may survive because the food they gave me here was pretty generous and good enough.

It was a lot better than what I was getting when I was working on the fields. I looked around the hospital, and all the other kids and an adult were in worse condition than I was. This also gave me hope. This place reminded me of the hospital that my grandmother was staying at before she passed away. That thick soup rice was pretty much their medicine for us. If you don't get well with the thick soup rice they gave you there, you probably would die.

My grandmother and uncle never got better and passed away.

I thought I was feeling better and recovering slowly because the food they gave me here was a big help to get my energy back. I kept thinking to myself that even if I was getting well, I would continue to act like I wasn't in order to stay here as long as I could. Because the food they gave me was decent, I would survive if I could stay here as long as they let me.

Even though the swelling in my stomach was getting better and I started to feel better, I found another problem within myself. I noticed that when I went to pee my testicles were also swollen up, and it felt like they were filled with water like a small balloon. That scared the hell out of me. I thought to myself "what the hell is going on with my body?" I thought I was feeling better already.

My testicles had swollen to the size of an egg on each side, and it was uncomfortable to walk, but I was too embarrassed to tell anybody yet what was happening to me. All I did for a few days was rest and hope that it would go away soon. So I kept this weird thing that had happened to me to myself for a while. Each day that went by I kept checking it and hoping that the swelling would go away, but it was getting bigger each day.

You have no idea how scared I was.

I had no idea what was wrong with me. I thought I was feeling better because the swelling on my body was coming down and the diarrhea had gone away, but the swelling on my testicles really had me worried. I was lonely, and I missed my family and this horrible thing was happening to me. I told myself that soon I would have to tell somebody about this or I may end up dead. I had no idea what caused this problem that I was having with my private parts. I had a plan to tell the person that gave me soup rice about my problem as soon as I got up in the morning. I could no longer keep this secret.

I went to bed that night feeling sorry for myself. When I woke up in the morning out of nowhere my mother came to this place to look for me. I could hear her voice in the long hallway talking to another person asking for me. Thank god she found me. I couldn't believe she found me and that she was alive all this time we were separated from each other. I thought I was dreaming.

I was incredibly happy to see my mother was alive and that she somehow, some way had found me. It was a miracle! It was unbelievable and amazing. I believe she stayed with me for a couple of days, long enough for me to tell her that I had this problem with my private parts and that I had been sick for a while now.

Once my mother took a look at my private parts and saw what had happened, she broke down and cried for a long time.

Mom didn't know what I had been through all this time I was away from her; it must have been at least six to eight months. Anyway, she was very concerned about what had happen to my private parts and wanted to know how this could have happened and what causes it. She couldn't believe I didn't tell anyone about this.

My mother, with or without my permission, was looking for some answers from some of the people that worked in the hospital. She wanted to find out what the hell was wrong with me. She was asking almost everyone to come and check out at my swollen private parts. You can imagine how embarrassed I was having this problem. Strangers, including men and women, were coming around to check me out.

I didn't have any choice but to go ahead and have everyone look at my testicles so I could get some help as soon as possible. There were no doctors or nurses there, and no one knew anything about medical conditions. When some of these people looked at my swollen testicles, they were shocked and said they had never seen anything like it. No one was able to come up with any solutions to the problem because no one had ever seen swollen nuts as big as mine; they were more like small balloons. It was the most ridiculous thing I have ever experienced. When I touched them the liquid inside seeped out and it hurt like hell. My pants would always get wet because of this.

The only thing my mother and the rest of the people could come up with was that my body severely lacked nutrition and vitamins to the point where it just started to swell up, especially my balls. It all made sense, but there was still no guaranteed answers to the problem. I was scared that I might die because of this problem, and no one was able to help me. I felt at anytime I could die because of this illness. Everyone around me was feeling sorry for me, even though some of them were in worse condition than I was. My mother told me to continue eating the food that they gave to me even if my body didn't want to take it because the food was decent and at least better than somewhere else.

I guess the hospital staff actually wanted our conditions to improve so we could get back to hard work again. My mother seemed to think that if I could eat something with a little more protein and vitamins than just soup rice and salty eggs that my condition would improve, and I would get better. I definitely agreed to that solution. After staying with me for several days, my mother had to go back to the place where she came from with my young brother before the Khmer Rouge came looking for her.

My mother told me that she would be back and would bring me some food like dry fish and other stuff that she could find. I asked her before she had to go if she was still living in the same area before they took me away? She told me they also moved her and my brother to a different area.

My mother told me the Khmer Rouge moved her and my younger brother far away from the place where I was at and she had to cross a small river to find me. With that said, my mother took off with my brother and headed back to her own village. I remember my mother told me that she went through quite a few villages in search for me and finally ran into this hospital and found me. It was almost like a miracle that she found me. She didn't think she would ever find me, and I didn't think I would ever see my mother again.

A few days went by and my mother was back to visit me again, this time without my younger brother. She left him at the village with other people who she trusted and knew would take care of him while she came to visit me. She brought me some pre-cooked fish in a small container and some dried fish wrapped in a plastic bag.

I was really pleasantly surprised to see my mother back and also to see that she had brought me some fish. I asked her how and where she got all this fish? All I remembered she told me was, it was not important how she got it. What was important was that I needed to eat as much of it as I could in order to get better.

I ate very well for a while because I had some pre cooked fish with my soup rice, and it was so good. I had some left over dry fish from my mother to store away under my bed for the next meal because she brought plenty. I told her to bring some back for my brother and herself, but she wouldn't. She insisted that I keep all of it for myself so I could have it for lunch and dinner the next week too

My mother left that same day before the sun set so she could be with my little brother at the village. She did not want to leave my brother with someone else for too long.

That night I went to bed with a full stomach, knowing that tomorrow I would also have dry fish to eat from the leftovers hidden under my bed. When I woke up in the morning I reached for the dry fish under my bed because I was excited that I had more left for lunch and dinner. It was going to taste so good again with the soup rice. To my surprise, all the dry fish hidden under my bed were gone! I looked everywhere under my bed but could not find them.

Someone had stolen all of my dry fish while I was asleep. I was so angry and disappointed that someone had done this. I needed this food to get better. I also thought that my mother was going to be angry that I let someone steal the dry fish from me. I knew then that my mother went through a lot to find these dry fish for me, and I let someone else take it away. I let my mother down by not taking care of the important food that was so hard to find.

Someone must have been watching me eating and putting the dry fish under my bed and decided to steal it at night while I was deep asleep. That was fine with me because I figured that I probably would do the same thing if I was so hungry and I saw that someone else had something more. So I went a few days without anything more than just the soup rice with salty eggs.

After getting used to eating the fish that mom had brought

me, the plain soup rice with salty eggs tasted pretty bad. I had become spoiled.

I continued to check my private parts every day, making sure it was not getting worse. It was still swollen up, but it stayed steady instead of getting bigger, and that was good news to me.

Several days later my mother was back bringing me more pre-cooked fish in a silver container and more dried fish. She immediately asked me whether I still had the dry fish that she brought for me earlier. I thought then I should lie to my mother so I wouldn't disappoint her, but I couldn't.

I told her the truth about what had happened to the leftover dry fish, and she was so angry with me for letting someone else steal it. I don't blame her, but this time my mother brought more dry fish and also some fresh red and green peppers. She thought the spices in the red and green peppers would help heal my swollen private parts. The dried fish my mother brought for me was called the snakehead, and it sometimes can be used as a medicine to cure some diseases because of the chemicals that it carries inside its body. That's what other people from the village told my mom.

My mother explained to me how difficult it was to find the snakehead fish, especially the ones that had been marinated and dried up. The red and green spicy peppers were also hard to find due to the shortage of it where she was living.

She continued to explain to me that it took a lot of effort for her to find these foods and she had to cross the river to bring them to me. She also told me that at one time she passed out in the middle of the road on her way to bring me this food because she was so tired from all the work that the Khmer Rouge forced her to do. Plus walking to the hospital took a lot out of her. The road from her village was long and rough. She told me over and over, at least three times that I remember, to be careful with the dried fish and other stuff that she had brought for me.

I felt bad after my mother told me what she went through to bring me that food, and I let someone else steal the remainder. My mother was a tough woman and a survivor through all of these ordeals, and I was the same way, a survivor too. I fought with everything I had because I wanted to live.

My mother continued to travel back and forth from her village to the hospital, bringing me food at least several times a week to make sure that I got enough to eat. I ate whatever she brought for me, including the spicy red and green peppers that were supposed to help heal my swollen private parts.

Even though the red peppers were almost unbearable for me to eat because they were so hot, I had to force myself to eat them because they might help bring down the swelling. They may also heal any other problems that I had. For a while I would have thick soup rice with dried fish and red peppers that mom brought for me. I built a certain level of tolerance for the red and green peppers, and they tasted pretty good after I got used to them.

I continued to have dried snakehead fish left over each day for the next week because mom had brought so much for me, but I never again let someone else steal them. I knew how valuable they were. Each night before I went to bed I would place the bag of dried fish between my legs and then cover myself with a blanket so no one would get it from me while I was asleep. I never put it under my bed again. I learned my lesson well.

Chapter 12

A few weeks later I noticed that the swelling on my nuts had come down significantly. I was starting to feel and look much better. I couldn't wait to tell my mother the next time she came back to see me. I honestly believe it was the nutrition and protein in the fish and the red and green peppers that helped me get better.

When my mother came back several days later she couldn't believe that I was healing and getting better. My private parts had healed significantly. Slowly, they were becoming normal again. I knew that my mother was a big part of why I was healing. To me my mother was a super woman who had been through a lot of hard times and never gave up in search for me. She spent a great deal of time and energy in search of food and other goods that had helped heal my illness. God must have helped my mother find me because it was impossible with all the places and villages around. Plus the Khmer Rouge was everywhere. Yet she never got caught all those times she brought me food. To me it was amazing how lucky we both were. As soon as my mother knew that I was feeling better, she was relieved and thankful.

She visited me less frequently once she knew that I was going to make it. She also had a commitment to take care of my younger brother. A short time after I recovered from my illness and everything was back to normal again, I continued to stay in the hospital because I was not ready to go back to suffering again on the rice fields.

Even though I was completely cured from my illness, I told the people in the hospital that I was still sick and I acted that way so they would believe me. They allowed me to stay in the hospital for an extended time. I stayed at the hospital for two reasons: they gave me a good amount of food to eat and I was able to see my mother. Surviving in any way I can was the key while I was in this ordeal.

Several months went by and I could no longer continue to pretend that I was sick. Some of the people there started to catch on. A short time later I found out that they were going to move me out of the hospital and to a different village because I was doing much better than other people there. That was a big surprise to me because I was not ready to move to a different village even though I was already well.

The thought of starving again in a different village scared me, plus if they were going to move me again, I would not be able to let my mother know where I was going. Nothing good could come out of moving to a different village; I'd been through it many times before. I was lucky to survive!

Since I was cured from my illness, my mother only visited

me once a week and there were no way of keeping in touch with her. I would not be able to tell my mother that the Khmer Rouge were going to move me to another village. When the Khmer Rouge forced me to move to a different village, I again lost contact with my mother. I could not believe I was separated from her again.

I'm not sure how my mother felt when she came to visit me in the hospital and found out that I was no longer there. She was probably as terrified as I was when I found out that I had to go away again. I always felt that once they moved me from one place to another that I was going to die or at least I would have to suffer from starvation again. The only reason that the Khmer Rouge forced you to move from one village to another was they wanted you to suffer and slave over work in the rice fields. If you were lucky enough to make it through that village, you were very lucky. They would move you to another village and the suffering would start all over again.

I believe the Khmer Rouge loved to see people suffer; it gave them power and control. As long as they could dictate the way things ran, they were happy.

The Khmer Rouge moved me into a new village somewhere in the countryside. My mother did not know where I was or what they were doing to me. As a kid I thought it was messed up what they had repeatedly done to my family and me. I was terrified each time they moved me from one place to another.

As soon as I figured out a way to survive in one village I had to start all over again. I felt like I was the only one they were doing this to, time after time, going from one place to another without my family. I continued to struggle from one village to another as they moved me around to wherever they wished.

I cannot believe that I was losing contact with my mother again after she had once found me. She must have been going crazy and maybe thought that I was dead, the same way she found out that my father was dead when they took him away from her. Anyway, while I was forced to be in this new village, my new job was to watch all the cows and buffalo out on the fields while they ate grass. Basically I was herding those water buffalos and cows. I had to make sure they didn't run away after they were done eating. I had to keep them under control and together at all times.

There must have been at least ten cows and five big water buffalo that I had to take care of, as well as some calves. The village where I was forced to live consisted of other adults and kids around my age, but more adults than kids as I remember. There were many people living in this part of the village, and there were lots of little huts everywhere.

This village was very interesting village, with many small huts, and we all stayed in a hut by ourselves. I appreciated the privacy. Maybe the other kids didn't like it as much as I did. I was used to being independent and staying by my self. I thought it was great to have a hut to myself and not have to share it with anybody else. Even though the hut was a small one, I liked it a lot.

My main job was to take care of all the calves, cows and buffalo. I had to make sure that they were fed and by the evening time, and I had to bring all of them back to the village where we lived. The Khmer Rouge counted how many cows and buffalo that I had to take care of and if some were missing at the end of the day, I would be in trouble. So each morning while the kids and adults were out on the wheat fields working I had to gather all the cows and buffalo and bring them out to the field where they could eat grass, wheat or whatever they could eat; I just needed to make sure that they were all full. By the evening I brought them all back to the village for the Khmer Rouge.

At first I thought there was no way that I could take care of all of those cows and buffalo all at the same time; they were huge animals, and I was just a kid. How was it possible to get them to go in one direction? All the cows and buffalo intimidated me, but I had to do whatever the Khmer Rouge told me to do. I'm not sure why they picked me to do that job and not the other kids, maybe because they thought that I was more alert than they were. The Khmer Rouge gave me a small whip to control the cows and buffalo, and off I went all by myself with a herd of cattle. The cows and buffalo were in two separate barns right next to each other, and the first time that I went to open the gate to let them out in the morning, they came rushing out like they knew they had to get out. I stayed as far away from the gate as possible so they would not run over me the minute I opened up the gate. These cows and buffalo actually almost knew where they needed to go for food once I let them out of the gate; they started walking out in separate group. The cows were in one group, and the buffalo were in another group.

All I had to do was lead them in the direction I wanted them to go, and they would all follow me, but sometimes I had to use my whip to do so. It actually really surprised me how easy it was to control these animals because they walked in groups, and it was almost effortless moving them toward the dry wheat field so they could eat grass and wheat.

Once I got them out on the grass part of the field, they just did their own thing and started eating the grass in groups, and all I had to do was find a shade nearby and sit and watch them eat. At first I found it intimidating having to control all of these animals at once. Once I got used to it and gained experience, it was quite easy, and I was having a good time taking care of them.

After a few days of herding the cattle, I really loved it, and it was very easy work for me to do. Sometimes I even got to ride the baby cows around the field while they ate, and sometimes I rode the big cows and buffalo too. That was how comfortable I was being around these cows and buffalo; they were harmless and tame as can be. The water buffalo were huge and their horns were scary, but they were just as tame as the cows.

I was very thankful that the Khmer Rouge chose me to

take care of their cows and buffalo while I was in this village. Even though I was a small, ten-year-old kid, the job the Khmer Rouge had me do was that of an adult. Actually it was a joy! At least I didn't have to go work out on the wheat fields planting rice and moving dirt and mud, which was to me far more difficult.

Before I knew it I got attached to these animals and I loved what I was doing. That was the only good thing that happened to me while living in this village. I felt alive and happy for the first time with these animals. Taking care of the cows and buffalo came easy to me. I was still not getting enough to eat each day, but I was surviving. It was the Khmer Rouge way while living here.

Each morning before taking the animals out for the day, I would look around the village to see if there was any leftover food for me to eat, but I found nothing. I was always the last one to leave the village each morning because I had to gather all the cattle together before leading them out onto the grass fields; that's why I was able to look around the village to see if I could find something to eat. I never could find any soup rice or rice left over from the night before, even in the area where the Khmer Rouge was staying, which was in the same complex believe it or not. The Khmer Rouge's huts were much bigger than ours, and they were located right in the middle of the village. I thought to myself "there's got to be some food left over somewhere in the village." I just had keep on searching everywhere.

So each morning I continued to search around the village for anything that I could find even around where the Khmer Rouge's huts were. By morning time everyone had left the village to work on the fields and sometimes the Khmer Rouge would also be gone. That left me with many opportunities to search around the village for food.

I was an exception to all their rules because I had a different job, and I felt that the Khmer Rouge started to like me. They thought that I was doing a good job of taking care of all the cows and buffalo for them. Even though I thought they liked me, I never got any extra foods, so I would always be hungry every day like all the other people in the village.

One day as I was searching around the village I noticed a small barn, and in that barn there were pigs, baby pigs and some chickens and roosters. The chickens were on one side of the barn while the pigs were on the other side, and when I saw this I was pleasantly surprised that there were other animals around besides the cows and buffalos. Across from the small barn was another big empty hut where no one lived. I thought that maybe some of the Khmer Rouge were living there, but every time I walked by to check, I saw no one.

So by this time I was excited because I saw some chickens and baby pigs in that barn and thought to myself that one night while everyone is asleep I would come down there and kill the baby pig with a knife and cut up the meat and cook it in the fire left from the big charcoal stove that the Khmer Rouge had used to cook up soup rice for us earlier in the evening. I thought big at that time because I was starving. I always had a plan and mostly about food. The charcoal fire in the stove usually lasted a long time, sometimes until early morning because it was so big. It had to be because cooking a big pot of soup rice requires lots of burning charcoal. Each night I saw the fire last until early morning even if nothing else was cooking on the stove. Well, it wasn't really a stove, but it was something like that.

My plan to kill the baby pig one night gave me hope and strength that soon I would have something meaty and tasty to eat. I had to figure out a way to kill the baby pig at night without the Khmer Rouge knowing about it. That was the hardest part for me. When you are starving everything seems to be possible and you will do whatever it takes to try and accomplish your mission you set out to do; that's how I felt. I would do whatever it took to find food.

All I wanted to do was to find a knife and kill that baby pig. For the next few days I spent part of my mornings in search of a knife so I could take care of the baby pig later. As I was looking around the village I came to an area where the Khmer Rouge left all their weapons, including several knives, lying around under the big huts. So I grabbed a small army knife and headed back to hide it under my hut before going on my way to feed the cows and buffalo on the fields.

Later that night, when everyone was asleep, I took off with the army knife and set out to kill the baby pig.

Once I got to the barn everything seemed to be very quiet. All the pigs and chickens were asleep, and I got excited and thought my plan was going to work and soon I would have real meat to eat. I moved forward slowly a step at a time and sneaked inside the barn so I wouldn't disturb the chickens and other big pigs that were right next to the baby one that I wanted to kill. I noticed that as I got closer to the baby pig I was stepping on the muddy area of the barn, and my feet were filled with mud.

I didn't like stepping on mud because it was going to make my attempt at killing the baby pig a little bit harder. Once I got to the baby pig I started to grab its neck with both of my hands to get it away from the mom so I could kill it, but the minute that I put both of my hands around the baby pig's neck it started to run away and making all kinds of weird noises, and that woke up the chickens on the other side of the barn.

Once the chickens were startled and awake all hell broke loose, and they made a lot of noise as they flew from one side to the other in a trance. By this time all the other big pigs woke up and caused all kinds of commotion, and I had to get out of that barn as fast as possible before I got caught. I knew trying to kill this baby pig wasn't going to be as easy as I thought it would be. I got out of that small barn as fast as I could. I feared that the Khmer Rouge might catch me because of all the noise that the chickens and pigs were making. With the army knife still in my pocket I made it back safely to my hut. I threw the knife under my pillow and pretended that I was asleep just in case someone had heard the noises. My heart was racing about a hundred miles per hour, knowing that the Khmer Rouge could have caught me. There was no way I could have killed that baby pig by myself, and even if I did kill it, how was I suppose to cut up the skin and the meat? The pigskin was very hard to penetrate even with a knife. How was I going to cook the meat without being caught?

I was only ten years old at the time, and that kind of major chore wasn't going to happen even though I thought I could do it. You could say that I was a crazy kid with all kinds of ideas about how to survive while starving in this village. I was again lucky that no one had noticed that I snuck out at night in search of the pig. The next day I went back to work herding cows and buffalo while craving all kinds of meat to eat, but there was none anywhere! I told myself I had to continue searching around the village for other things to eat before I starved to death.

What they gave us was never enough to eat. So I continue my search around the village each morning before heading out to the field with the cows and buffalos. One day as I was walking around the village after work I saw a group of Khmer Rouge sitting around eating cooked fish on an open fire. They were talking, laughing and eating fish by their huts. So I thought must be some leftover fish around where they were because they were cooking them and eating them in front of us, yet they would never give us any to eat. I was deprived of food.

As I walked around their big huts one morning I discovered a small dug up barrel, like hole covered with a lid, so I went up to it and removed the lid to see what was in it. To my surprise it contained many fish that the Khmer Rouge kept just for themselves. The fish in this barrel were all alive. The light bulb came on over my head again, and ideas started flashing inside about what to do next.

I decided to come back for some of these fish at night while everyone was asleep. I had to lay low for a while and make sure that when I decided to come back and steal the fish, no one would be around. So I would walk back and forth past this area several times a night just to make sure of the safest time to come. I did not want to get caught doing this.

I was very hungry and couldn't wait to go ahead and do this at night. All I wanted was to eat one of those fish. Several days later, after I carefully thought out a plan, I took off around midnight. Once I got to the area where I saw the barrel of fish, I started to pray: "please let there be fish left in this barrel so I can steal them, and please god don't let anyone see me doing it." This all happened before I tried to open the lid of the barrel.

I wanted those fish so badly that I was willing to even eat them raw if I didn't have any way of cooking them. That was how starving I was.

I looked around to make sure there wasn't anybody around before I proceeded to open the lid of the barrel. The minute I opened the lid, some of the fish started to jump up trying to get out of the barrel. I was so happy that there were some fish left over in this barrel. I put the lid down and grabbed one with both of my hands, and once I got a hold of it, I started to twist its neck with my right hand to try and kill it. I killed the fish with both of my young hands, and I didn't even have to use the knife that I brought with me just in case. The fish wasn't that big, maybe eight inches long. It was a snakehead fish as I recall.

I took the dead fish, which wasn't very big, and rolled it in my pants around the waist. I closed the lid back on the barrel and took the fish that I had stolen back to my hut. When I got back to my hut I was so excited knowing that I had this fish with me, my heart was beating like a drum. So I sat there in my hut with the dead fish still in my pants trying to gather myself and calm down so I could go back out and cook it in the fire that was still burning nearby. I was the only kid up and awake, everyone was asleep.

When I settled down, I took the fish and stuck it in the nearby burning charcoal, but it started to go out by the time I got there. A few minutes later the charcoal fire died out, so I took the fish out from the charcoal and brought it back to my hut and began tearing the skin out and eating the meat that I desperately needed. The first three or four bites tasted incredible, but then I noticed that it wasn't fully cooked, but it didn't matter to me. I finished it up anyway, cooked or not.

Once I ate all the meat on the fish, I dug a little hole by my hut and buried the bones and skin so no one would see the evidence. I have no idea where the Khmer Rouge got all those fish, but they filled up the barrel everyday with snakeheads. I didn't care where they got them. I was just glad to see them everyday, and there would be plenty of left over after they were done with them. However, I continued to steal fish from the Khmer Rouge at night without getting caught, but I didn't do it every night. I would go out and steal the fish every other night.

I told myself if I was to do it every night it would be too often, and my chance of getting caught by the Khmer Rouge would be much greater. Plus I didn't need to eat the fish every night. A couple of times a week was plenty to keep me alive without getting caught. So when I found out that I could steal these fish and cook them at night and eat them without getting caught, I began to feel much better and have more strength. Each day I went to work taking care of the cows and buffalo. I didn't need any rest like I did before and I was able to run with the cows and buffalo. I even had enough energy to jump on top of the water buffalo's back to ride on it instead of waiting for it to lie down.

Chapter 13

One day I was riding on one of the water buffalo's backs while watching the other cows and buffalo eating wheat and grass I noticed a larger water buffalo from far away, and it wasn't the water buffalo in my group I was taking care of. I believe this water buffalo was a male, and it was huge. Even from far away it looked big, and it started to run toward my group of buffalo, getting faster as it got closer. I was so scared as it got closer to the buffalo that I was riding on, and it wasn't slowing down at all, so I jumped off the back of my buffalo and started running toward tree as fast as I could.

I climbed up on the nearest tree that I could find and sat there on one of the tree branches and hung on for my life. Watching from the top of the tree, I saw the bull was chasing my group of buffalo and cows to another field, and then it finally stopped and started to circle around my group of buffalos. All of a sudden I saw the bull got on top of one of my female buffalos and start to do its thing. I guess it was just a male buffalo in heat, and I got caught in the middle of it.

When the bull was done, it started to chase the other male buffalo that were in my group for a very short time, and then it took off. At first I was terrified by this charging male buffalo and thought that I was going to die before finding a tree to climb, and then I found it entertaining to watch the water buffalo doing the dirty. I never thought I could climb a tree that fast until that day of the incident with the water buffalos. After the dominant male buffalo left and everything had calmed down, I got off the tree and ran over to another field where all my cows and buffalo were and started counting them to see if I had lost any of them to the rampage, but I was lucky that all of them had stayed together. If I would have lost any of the cows or water buffalo, I was sure to be in trouble with the Khmer Rouge, and they probably would not let me take care of the cows and buffalo again.

The thought of that really scared me because I really liked what I was doing, and I was good at it; it was easy for me, and I was surviving. Every day I was out on the field with these animals I was having fun, and I got to ride on their backs all the time. I believe that if I had worked on the wheat fields planting rice, moving dirt and mud from one area to another to form walkway for the Khmer Rouge, especially with the kind of food they were giving me, I would not have made it. I probably would have died from overwork and starvation, like some of the other people in the village. I guess I was somewhat lucky that the Khmer Rouge chose me to do a certain job that kept me alive, but I also had to steal a lot from them to stay alive.

While they forced me to move to this village and herd cows

and buffalo, I honestly felt like someone was looking out for me. It was the perfect job for me to stay alive.

The Khmer Rouge forced me to live in this village for quite some time. Even though I missed my family and always wondered where they were, I was doing ok by myself. I was surviving because I was stealing fish from The Khmer Rouge and they hadn't caught me. I believed I was blessed. After about six months of living in this village the Khmer Rouge once again decided to announce that they would have to move some of us to different area soon.

The last thing I wanted to hear from them was I have to move again, because I was doing so well in this part of the village herding cows and buffalo. Each time that I was forced to move to a different area, I had to struggle to survive. This village so far had been good to me. I wished that they would keep me there to continue taking care of the cows and buffalo.

Most people in this village were struggling to survive due to the harsh working conditions that the Khmer Rouge put them in and also the lack of foods. I was doing much better than most people there because I was lucky to have the easy job of taking care of the animals, and also because I was fortunate not to get caught stealing from the Khmer Rouge at night. Most people did not want chance stealing from the Khmer Rouge because they didn't want to get caught and pay the ultimate price, death. To me, starving to death would be the same result. Some just did not know where to steal.

I would rather take my time planning the best way to steal from them without getting caught. I also prayed hard that I would not get caught. However, if I was to get caught stealing, I was ready to deal with the consequences. I would rather do this than slowly and painfully starve to death; it's not the way that I wanted to go.

When it was time for The Khmer Rouge to move people again, I was among the ones to go. As disappointed as I was, I had no other choices but to move when they ordered me to. I thought I had a chance to stay in this village and continue to take care of the cows and buffalo because the Khmer Rouge seem to like me and what I did for them. But that wasn't the case because the next day I was ordered again to go with the other small group of people to a different village.

We walked for hours before reaching another village. This, as it turned out, was where I reunited with my mother, sister and brother. They moved me to the village where my family was. I was shocked and surprised to see them in this village. They were also very surprised that I was moved there to that village. I was lucky to be reunited with my family.

For some odd reason the Khmer Rouge also moved my sister to this village from where she was. I don't believe they planned for us to reunite there; it just happened because there were too many people for them to keep track of. In this village, we actually got to live together as a family again. Finding each other again for the first time in months was like a miracle

Chapter 14

The year was 1977, and we were brought together once again, albeit by accident, by the Khmer Rouge. The chance of this happening was slim, but it happened. We were all living in a small hut together in this village, along with some other people who was forced here. Our hut had ladder leading up to it about ten feet high. So each night we had to climb up the ladder to get into our hut to sleep.

There was a man staying right next to our hut, and he had four big water buffalo. He was looking for someone to take care of them for him. When I heard that he was looking for a person to take care of his water buffalo, I told mom that I had done this before at another village. Actually, I told mom that I had taken care of many cows and water buffalos.

I explained to my mother that I had the experience, and if that man wanted I could take care of his four buffalo no problem. Basically I was asking my mom to talk with this man. I was not sure whether the man was Khmer Rouge or one of us, but I didn't care because I wanted to take care of the water buffalo.

I knew I could do a good job and it would be a way for me to get out of working out in the wheat fields again. So before

I knew it my mother approached the man and told him that I wanted to take care of his water buffalo and that I had done it before in another village. The man agreed. My job was to take the water buffalo out to the field each morning and feed them, let it play in the water and run around the field, feed them again in the afternoon and take them back before evening. Although these four water buffalo were huge, they were very tame and laid back animals once I figured out their behavior.

In the meantime my mother and sister were ordered to work on the other side of the village. My mother and sister were also very lucky that the Khmer Rouge had them work separating wheat from the rice instead of working out on the field planting them. They were among the few chosen to stay in the village and work; it was lighter and easier work than out on the fields for sure. It was still hard work, but not quite as hard as working on the fields.

The work my mother and sister did was still hard, but it was tolerable. They also got to work in the shade. My younger brother sometimes went to work with my mother and sister, but he did not have to work because he was so young. While I was out all day taking care of the buffalo for the man next door, my mother and sister were at the village near by separating wheat from rice using a manual tool provided by the Khmer Rouge. As far as food was concerned nothing had changed. They gave us small portions of soup rice twice a day. I know this is repetitious, but it was true. We were all deprived of real food. One thing really helped us though. Whenever the Khmer Rouge was not around, my mother and sister would steal some rice, a little bit at a time from where they worked. My mother would cook the rice and feed us a little bit at a time each day to help keep us from starving. The hardest part was to cook the rice and not let the Khmer Rouge know about it. When they were around the area we couldn't cook it until they were gone. Sometimes my mother and sister would work with corn too, using a machine to smash the corn and turning it into flour. Whenever there was an opportunity, my mother and sister would also steal some corn. (It was a bold move on their part, but they did it).

My mother would always hide the rice bag from my brother and me. She knew that if we found out where she put it, we would eat it all. Sometimes she would hide the bag in the corner of the hut. She covered the small bag of rice with several pieces of clothing to make it look like it was just a pile of clothing, but I knew better because I had stolen many things before. I was the expert! When I found out where she had hidden the bag of rice, I went crazy and started eating it raw because I was so hungry.

Sometimes I would even come home to the hut early to eat the raw rice she got at home. That was how hungry I was in this village. There was other food in this area of the country. Sometimes I would find a few small crabs here and there from the field, but that was not enough to keep me from being hungry everyday.

Shortly after I found where my mother hid the bag of rice, my brother found it too. I believe he was eating the raw rice too. I can tell you that the raw rice did not taste good; actually it was kind of milky once I got it all chewed up. I think the reason my mother hid the raw rice from me and my brother was because she wanted to save some of it for later when we really desperately needed it. This was a good idea, but I couldn't wait, and neither could my brother because we were always hungry.

One thing my mother did not know was that I was used to finding hidden things. So finding the rice my mother was trying to hide from me was almost too easy. One day, my mother caught my brother in the act of eating the raw rice. She saw him put the raw rice in his mouth as she came home from work. She started to yell at him and scared him really bad to the point where he tried to run away, but instead he fell down the ladder and hit his head on the rungs, cracking his head about several inches.

When he landed on the ground, my mother came down to see if he was ok. My brother was bleeding pretty badly from the head, so my mother decided to take him to see the people nearby and ask for their help. She took my brother to see a woman who gave him a homemade medicine made out of tree leaves and other bitter dried fruits that helped stop the bleeding. She put the homemade medicine on top of my brother's head, where the cut was, to stop the bleeding.

After a few minutes, the homemade medicine worked like

magic, and the bleeding stopped. My mother asked the woman what was in that medicine. The woman told my mother it contained dried bitter fruits mashed with some sesame seed and green tree leaves. From then on my mother would know how to make this homemade medicine just in case someone else got hurt. Thank god for the help of that woman.

My mother made a prayer, thanked the woman for her help, and took my brother back home. When she got my brother home, she asked him why he ate the raw rice? He told my mother that he was too hungry and could not wait for her to cook it. She also told him not to ever try to run down the ten-foot ladder again. It scared her really bad when he fell. She thought he might have killed himself.

I will tell you honestly that every night I went to bed hungry. There wasn't enough rice or anything else to eat. I continued to steal the rice out of the bag. I would then eat it raw at night to fill my hunger, even though it didn't taste very good. That was still not enough; it was only raw rice, and I felt horrible afterward.

I usually slept right next to the bag of rice and would take a handful to eat every night, until one night my mother caught me stealing the rice too. As I was trying to reach for the bag, my mother happened to be up and caught my hand, and I was doomed. She asked me what I was doing. She caught me red handed, so I told her I was starving and needed to eat these raw rice. She couldn't believe that I was also stealing rice and eating it raw. What my mother didn't know was that I was the first one to eat the raw rice. So from that day on, my mother would cook the rice a little bit more when she got a chance to so my brother and I would not have to eat the raw rice again. However, she could only cook the rice when the Khmer Rouge was not around.

Anyway, my brother and I started to get swollen stomachs from eating too much raw rice, and we both had to stop eating the raw rice after mom had found out.

Chapter 15

One day while I was out herding cattle, when I heard lots of big loud explosions in the distance. It sounded like bombs and gunshots going off. Then I saw people running back to the village, yelling and screaming, so I gathered the four water buffalo and decided to head back to the village too. I was scared because I had no idea what was going on. When I got to the village I noticed people were running away carrying their belongings. I found my mom, sister and brother waiting for me there.

I asked my mom what was going on. She told me we have to get out of there as soon as possible. The man who owned the buffalos told me the same thing. He said everybody must leave this village as soon as possible because there was fighting going on at that moment. As I gave him back his four water buffalo, the man offered me one of his bulls.

I thought it was awesome that I could take this water buffalo with us. I was attached to those water buffalo anyway, and this was a great gift. I asked my mother if I could take the water buffalo with us, and I promise her if she let me I would take good care of it. She said no because we would not have time to drag this big animal with us. We had to move as fast as we could to get away from these bombings. We couldn't take the water buffalo along with us. I was devastated when my mother said no to the buffalo because I loved this animal and had grown attached to it. I had to say good-bye to this beautiful buffalo and its owner. I believe this man was one of us; otherwise he wouldn't have been so nice to my family and me.

As soon as we said goodbye to the man and his four buffalo, we packed our bags and left the village with other people. We ran as fast as we could while carrying some bags in our hands. People were running along the country road next to each other, shoulder to shoulder. Children were crying and adults were yelling in fear for their lives as the bombs and gunshots continued to go off in the background. The explosions were so loud that we thought the bombs could hit us at anytime! So we continued to run. When we got too tired, we would walk for a little while then run again. Basically we followed the crowd of people.

We continued to walk and run for what seemed like a whole day. I was running next to my mother and sister, and the next thing I knew, I was running next to someone else because there were so many people running in one direction, and it was dusty. I thought my family would catch up with me soon. I continued to run for a while along with other people, but I never saw my mother, sister and brother as I kept on looking back. I was scared.

As we moved further and further on, people started to

spread out quite a bit, and some disappeared into the distance. All of a sudden there were fewer and fewer people running behind me. I started to yell out for my mother, sister and brother, but no one would answer. I kept on running, but I was getting tired to the point where my running turned into walking. Then I had to stop because I was too exhausted.

I sat in the middle of the road next to the wheat field, waiting for my family and hoping that they would show up soon. I started to scream at the top of my voice trying to get somebody's attention, because I was alone in the middle of the road next to all the wheat fields. I don't know how I lost everyone but I did. I was scared, hungry and tired all at the same time, and it was started to get dark. By this time, I no longer heard any bombs going off and no gunshots. Maybe we had moved so far away from the bombs that we could no longer hear them or maybe they decided to stop the bombings for a while, I'm not sure. I just knew it was quiet.

As we found out later, those bombs, grenades and gunshots were from the North Vietnamese soldiers trying to take over the east side of our country. Those bombings, in turn drove the Khmer Rouge into the jungle.

Anyway, I was alone, and it was getting dark as I continue to yell out for my family or anybody to come and get me, but no one had heard me. The only voice I heard back was the echo of my own voice, which sounded creepy. I continued to yell until I could no longer yell and I lost my voice. By this time it was almost dark, and I figured that I had to keep on walking or no one would ever find me.

I continued to walk ahead following the road that I hoped would lead me to someone. I remember looking up at the sky, crying to myself and praying that I would find someone soon because I was so tired and hungry. I kept on walking alongside the small road by the wheat fields. There were wheat fields to the left and right side of the road, and, because I was so tired, I kept on stepping on the muddy part of the road and almost falling off onto the wheat field.

A short time later, I found myself tripping on my own feet, and I fell right into the wheat field and got myself all wet. When I turned around to try to get out, I saw a couple of dead bodies lying in the middle of the wheat field, not too far from where I was. This terrified me. One body was swollen up pretty big facing down, and the other one had a plastic bag over the head. As you can imagine, I freaked out and got out of the wheat field and started running along the roadside stepping on the mud and everything. As I was running away from what I'd seen, I thought, "I'm going to die here, and no one will ever find me again."

I told myself I didn't want to die this way, all by myself struggling. I continued to run ahead in fear and finally passed out in the middle of the road somewhere. When I woke up, I saw two men looking down at me and shaking my shoulders. I guess they were trying to wake me up. Once they saw that I was awake, they began to ask me questions: what was I doing here all by myself? How did I get here?

When I woke up and saw those two men, I thought I saw god. I was so happy that I saw someone there with me. I didn't care whether they were Khmer Rouge or not, I just wanted to see someone for my sake. Anyway, I told the two men that I was running away with my family from all the bombings and somehow got lost, and that was how I ended up here all by myself. The two men looked at me and said that they were also running away from the bombings, and that everyone had settled down not too far away. They also told me the only reason that they were here was to hunt for food. I told the two men that I was happy to see them, I and asked them if they could bring me to see my family. They told me that they would help me get back to where all the other people had settled down, and that I might find my family there. In the meantime, I was hungry, and the two men gave me a piece of meat to eat; it tasted so good. I asked them what kind of meat that was because I had never tasted anything like it before. They told me it was rat meat. They had killed it earlier and cooked it. I was shocked because it tasted so delicious. I really didn't care what kind of meat it was because I was starving. The two men told me that I was very lucky that they found me. I could have woken up and started walking the wrong way and found no one around. I agreed completely.

One of the men ended up carrying me to the place where everyone had settled. Once we got there, the two men were

When I finally saw the hole, I was excited and immediately started digging with my stick. I dug for a long time, as it supposed to lead the way to the rat. I thought to myself that this really sucked. The hole wasn't really deep at all; it just ran along the ground maybe about five to six inches deep.

Finally, after digging for what seemed like twenty minutes, I saw a rat's tail. I thought it was awesome! My first chance at killing a rat. I grabbed the rat's tail and held on to it real tight, pulling it out of the hole as fast as I could. Once it was out, I started to bash it on the ground repeatedly until I was sure it was completely dead. I had killed my first rat, and it was a pretty good size rat too. It must have been at least six inches long not counting the tail and it was nice and fat one. That poor rat!

I put the dead rat in the bag and turned around to look at the hole to double check, making sure that there weren't any more rats in the hole. As I looked at the hole closely, I saw another rat's tail just barely sticking out. I continued to dig a few more inches, and there it was, another rat in that same hole. I pulled it out and killed it the same way and put it in the bag. I looked at the hole again and saw another tail. By this time I was having great fun, and I was amazed that there were three rats in the same hole. That was awesome!

I pulled it out, killed it and put it in the bag. I thought there might be more rats in this hole. I looked at the hole again and there was another tail I could see sticking out of the same hole. While I killed this one, I thought maybe there were more rats that ran in this hole. So I kill the fourth rat and put it in my bag, feeling confident that I would find another one in the same hole. As I looked to check the hole again, I saw no more rats' tails within sight. Just to make absolutely sure that there were no more rats in this hole, I continue to dig a few more inches until I reached the end of the hole.

The first hole I dug up, I found and killed four good-sized rats. I continued to dig holes and killed more rats all day long. I had so much fun, although it was hard work. By the end of my first day, I had half a bag of dead rats to take back home for my family. I was excited and couldn't wait to show my mother what I had. When I got back to the hut, I told my mother what I had in the bag. She opened it and was immediately shocked that there were that many rats in the bag. There must have been at least twenty-five rats. My mother was surprised that I could go out and kill that many rats by myself at the age of ten years.

What I thought funny was that I didn't have to tell my mother what the rats were for; she immediately knew they were our food. My mother and sister were ecstatic to see we would have meat to eat. They were the ones who gutted and cleaned the rats. They kept the hearts and livers and cooked them along with the meat.

The first time I ate cooked rats' meat, it tasted unbelievably delicious and sweet. I know it sounds really horrible, but believe me, the rats were good rats honestly. When I say good rats, I mean they were not poisonous or dirty like the city rats. All these rats ate was wheat out in the countryside, and they were healthy rats, believe it or not. Eating rats' meat was a blessing, and it saved our lives.

From this point on I hunted for rats everyday in different parts of the dry fields. As time went by, I gained more experience hunting and sometimes I would bring home a full bag of dead rats by the end of the day. It also got easier for me once I knew exactly where to look for the holes. The best place to look for these holes was on even dried ground. Some days were easier than others. Sometimes I would have two bags full of rats to take back home at the end of the day. The only way that I could carry the two bags of rats home was to tie each bag up with string and hook them to each end of a six-foot wooden stick. I then carried the wooden stick over my shoulders with a bag hanging from each end of the stick.

We would have rats to eat basically every day, and they became our main source of food. My mother would sometimes marinate the rats with salt. Then she sun dried them for a couple of days so we could keep them for longer periods of time. We all did not have to deal with the Khmer Rouge while we lived here because for the most part the North Vietnamese soldiers had forced them into the jungle part of our country. The only thing we had to worry about was searching for food, and I had mastered ways to hunt rats, we were well fed, and water from the nearby lake kept us from being thirsty.

Chapter 16

A few months went by, and my brother started to have problems with his eyes; sometimes he could not see well at night. His vision got to the point where he could barely see at all, especially at night. My mother was very concerned and wondered what was happening to his vision.

She took my brother around the area to see if anybody knew anything about my brother's eye problem. No one seemed to know why all of a sudden my brother was losing his eyesight. It was frightful to all of us, especially my brother. Finally my mother met an old woman who seemed to know what was wrong with my brother. She told my mother that my brother was losing his eyesight because he lacked nutrition and vitamins, most importantly iron. She told my mother to cook lots of rats' livers for my brother to eat each day, and that should help his eyesight.

When my mother came back to our little hut, she started to cook lots of rat livers for my brother to eat. She would fry the livers because that was the easiest way to prepare them. None of us would eat any of the livers from that point on; they would all be saved for my brother to eat to help regain his vision. We ran out of livers quickly because each rat only has one liver, and they were small because the rats were small.

One day I overheard several men talking about hunting for the bigger rats at night from the tree, so I went up to them and asked if I could go with them to hunt at night too. At first they told me I was too young, and then they kind of laughed at me jokingly. I, on the other hand, was very serious about going out hunting for the bigger rats at night for my brother sake. I told the men that I was serious.

I told the men that my brother had lost his eyesight and could not see at night and needed to eat as many rats' livers as possible. There were no animals around except the rats. I didn't have any other choices, like chickens, pigs or anything else to kill. I begged the men to please let me go with them to hunt at night. I assured them that I could do this and keep up with them because I had killed rats many times before.

They still could not believe that I wanted to go with them that badly, but they finally said yes. They had told me that I would need a bag, a sharpened stick and a flashlight. They told me to meet with them after sunset at the hut where they were staying. I was very happy they let me go hunting with them. I ran back to our hut and told my mother that I would like to go hunting with these other men. My mother approved and told me that I could go because we needed as many rats as we could possibly get.

So that same day I sharpened my stick to the point where it

was extra sharp to get ready for the nighttime hunting. I asked my mother for the flashlight so I could use it to kill the rats in the trees. I don't remember where my mother got the flashlight from, but she had one for me to use. With everything I needed in my possession, I was ready to go meet up with the men for the thrill kill. Once the sun had set and it was getting darker, I met up with the men at their hut. Then I followed them out to where we needed to go. There were two men and no other kids except myself. We walked about half an hour to get to the area where all the big trees were, and we settled in to hunt for the big rats. As we all got to the area where the trees were, the two men told me to be very quiet when I might scare away the rats. We had to be stealthy around the trees. The men also told to me the best way to kill these rats was to shine the flashlight directly at their eyes; the rat will freeze up once they saw our light. Then take the sharpened stick and stab it in the gut as hard as possible; most of the time it will die with one good hard stab to the right area. Once killed it can then be put in the bag. One of the men told me to be very careful because sometimes a rat can turn around and bite if it's not dead yet.

After he was done explaining the killing procedures to me, he told me to go to a different tree to look for the rats. Each one of us went to a different tree. I walked around and shone my flashlight at several trees before I came in contact with a big rat hanging out on one of the tree branches. I was actually scared the first time I saw this big rat hanging on the tree branch. It was more like a possum than a rat because it was so big and nasty looking.

It was just hanging out there on the tree branch with my light shining directly at it. I took the sharpened stick in my right hand and stabbed it straight in the stomach and let go of the stick. I jumped back several feet and watched the big rat fall to the ground. It moved around for several minute like it was trying to get away from the stick in its stomach. Instead of getting away the rat was dying from the massive wound. I had me a dead rat on the stick.

After it stopped moving I walked slowly over to the stick and removed the big dead rat from it. I then took it over to one of the men to show them that I had killed my first big rat. They couldn't believe that a small kid like me could kill a rat that big. This rat must have been at least three to four pounds. The men were impressed and told me to continue hunting and see if I could kill any more big rats. My first night of hunting for those rats, I took home three big ones. When I took the dead rats home that night, my mother, sister and brother did not believe that I killed those big rats all by myself. I couldn't believe it myself.

My Mother immediately gutted and cleaned them up and cooked them. Since those rats were much bigger than the field rats, their livers and hearts were also much bigger; mom saved them all for my brother. Since my brother needed to eat as many livers as possible in order to regain his vision, I needed to go out hunting for the smaller rats during the day time and the bigger rats during the night time. After many days of rat killing, both days and nights, we had many left over, even after mom sun dried lots of them. We ended up sharing many of these rats with some people who lived near us. They were happy and appreciative that we shared the rats with them. I got to the point where I was looking forward to going out each day and night in search of rats because I really enjoyed it.

I got really good at hunting for these creatures and it felt great! We were eating well too.

I remembered a time when I was out during the day digging holes on the dry field in search for rats and ran into a snake instead. I was digging along and following the hole to get to the rat. I pulled one rat out, killed it and put it in my bag. I looked in the hole to see if there was another one waiting for me, and instead of a rat, I saw a huge snake. As soon as I saw the snake, I grabbed my bag and ran as fast as I could to get away from it. The snake chased me for a while when I first started to run because when I looked back, it was right behind me. I was frightened, and I ran faster. A few moments later, it disappeared.

The man who showed me the proper way of hunting for rats was absolutely right! Sometimes you will run into a snake while attempting to kill rats and you have to be very careful. Sometimes the snake would go into the rat's hole to wait for it to come in. I hated snakes, and every time that I happened to see one, I would run faster than a horse to get away from it. Actually for me, hunting at night was just as fun as doing it during the day, maybe a little bit more challenging.

My brother's vision was getting a little bit better after continuously eating the rat livers. I mean he was eating livers like there was no tomorrow. Thank god that my brother really liked livers. Actually there was no other food for him to compare it to, so he had to like it. After a few weeks of eating nothing but rat livers, he began to see a little bit clearer at night, which made us very happy.

It was a big relief for me as well because I was doing something good for my brother. I believe after about one month of eating rat livers, my brother's vision was back to normal, and he was able to see at night like everyone else. For some special reason, these rat livers worked like a medicine, and they cured my brother's vision problem.

My brother never had problems with his eyes again. Hence my mother, sister and I started to eat rat livers as well. Not only did the livers provide a good source of iron for our bodies, but we also thought they tasted very good. The place where we were living was out in an open area in the middle of a big dry land, so each day was hot and humid. When it got too overbearingly hot and humid, we would all go to the small lake nearby and cool down for a little while.

The hot and dry weather was also good for us because my mother and sister could use the hot sun each day to dry left over rats so we could keep them for longer periods of time, kind of like rat jerky. Once all the rats were completely dried out from the sun, we put them in a bag and kept them for a long time. Whenever we needed to eat it, all we had to do was take a rat out of the bag and stick it over the fire for a few minutes, and it would be ready to eat. To us it was kind of like a rat jerky except we had to cook it a little bit before we could eat it. My mother had several bags of rat jerky saved up after a few months of living here. While living here in this wide-open area of the countryside, we had it pretty good; there was no Khmer Rouge to control us and we felt a sense of freedom for a short time. Although we had nothing with us while living there, we could hunt for rats and other things like fish and crabs. We ate mostly rats because I could get so many of them; for other people, it was crabs and fish. For those of us whose main source of food was the rats, small and big, it was the best. They tasted better than fish and more of them were available to us. There was nothing that would come close to the taste of cooked rat meat. Most of the people around us would agree with. Some people, while living here, had to hunt for something else because they were not successful at hunting for rats. They would settle for small fish and small crabs instead; sometimes would not be enough, and they would suffer and get very sick to a point where some even died of starvation.

After about six months of living there, most of us have felt comfortable enough to call this place our temporary home, as long as there were no Khmer Rouge to run our lives. We also knew that we wouldn't be able to live there forever just surviving off rat meat. One day we'd have to get out of this place and try to go somewhere else, closer to the city. In the meantime, we were stuck here, our temporary home in the middle of nowhere.

Chapter 17

One day, we went to the lake with some other people to take a bath and to bring water back to our little huts. On our way back we heard bombs going off again. After so many months of quiet things seemed to have settled down, but the bombs were coming down again, and it sounded like it was really close. The minute we heard the bombs, we rushed back to our huts and packed our belongings and prepared to leave as soon as we could. Other people did exactly the same thing. The fighting had started again.

People panicked and scattered around the wide-open area. We all panicked. It felt like the bombs could hit us at any time. We packed our belongings and some food, including some left over rice that mom had kept. We waited until everyone else was ready, then we followed them out of the area. I believe we were running, west away from all the bombs going off in the east side of the country.

Not knowing where in the world we all were headed, we continued to follow the crowd of people, hoping that it would lead us somewhere safe. We wished and prayed for our safety as we ran along the roadside carrying our belongings. To me it felt like we ran and walked for days trying to get as far away from the bombs as possible. It caused our adrenalin to kick in.

As the sun has set that evening, we came to rest at another small abandoned village. No one was there except all of us who ran away from the bombs. We were too tired to move on any further. We could still hear the bombing, but it was so far away now that we felt safe enough to stop and rest at least for the night. As soon as we have reached this abandoned village, we ate the rice that mom brought from the previous place. We were all so very tired that we could barely move. Once we were done eating, we crashed at this village for the night.

When we woke up in the morning, all the bombings had stopped, and it was quiet again. It was time to move on again. We gathered all of our belongings and decided we must keep on going. We continued to walk with the crowd to wherever they lead us to. Once again I felt like we must have walked all day long, until we all finally became very tired and came to rest in the middle of the road somewhere in the countryside.

I'm not sure where we were, but I know we were resting on the roadside. We were all too tired to move and too tired to go anywhere else. We decided we should all sleep there for the night. We were very fortunate that mom had brought some rat jerky with her. We ended up cooking the rat jerky for dinner that night. We also shared it with some other people near us.

When we came to rest on the roadside that night; there was a man who had two sons with him resting across from us. All of the other people who ran with us also came to rest on the roadside for many blocks. We decided that since we were so far away from all the bombings, we would be safe to stay in this place to rest for a few more days.

We had to recoup and regain our strength back in order to move on again. The next morning, the two sons who were staying across from us decided that they were going to head out to look for food. They set out that morning, and they went far away. I did not know why they decided to do this.

This turned out to be fatal for one of the brothers. Without knowing where they were headed, the two got closer to the jungle, and that was when they got into big trouble. As the two brothers were searching around for food, they unfortunately ran into some Khmer Rouge. When the Khmer Rouge saw the two brothers from a distance, they started shooting at them with their rifles. The two brothers ran away from the Khmer Rouge the minute that they saw them shooting. As the two brothers ran away one got shot and went down. The Khmer Rouge captured him a short time later. The other brother had no other choices except to continue to run; otherwise he would be captured too. He ended up hiding in a nearby lake filled with water lilies.

He covered his head with water lilies so the Khmer Rouge would not see him if they decided to come look for him around the lake. In the meantime, he could hear his brother pleaded with the Khmer Rouge. The Khmer Rouge would have no mercy on his brother. He could hear his brother scream with horror as the Khmer Rouge tortured him.

The Khmer Rouge eventually killed his brother. After the Khmer Rouge killed the brother, they came looking for him. They saw two people running away from them. They circled around the lake talking to each other but couldn't see the other brother hiding under the water lilies. A few minutes later, the Khmer Rouge took off without having seen the surviving brother.

After waiting for a long time to make sure that the Khmer Rouge was gone, the surviving brother got out of the lake and ran over to his dead brother. The Khmer Rouge left the dead brother lying there in the middle of the field. When the surviving brother got to his dead brother, he saw that the Khmer Rouge had carved out both of his brother's eyeballs and stuffed the eye sockets with grass. This was beyond evil and unimaginable.

The Khmer Rouge must have kept his brother's eyeballs because he did not see them around where his brother was killed. That was how cruel and dangerous these Khmer Rouges were. They could torture you in ways you can never imagine possible. He had to carry his dead brother back to the place where we all were staying to show his dad and everyone around what the Khmer Rouge had done. He also wanted to warn all of us that some of the Khmer Rouge was still in this area.

Everyone flocked around the dead brother and sobbed,

including his dad. Everyone was shocked at what they had seen. It was not possible that a human being could do this to another human being. We didn't know what was happening until later because people had already surrounded the father and his two sons to take a look at what the Khmer Rouge had done. Once people had moved away, we finally got a chance to look at the dead brother.

I was there and had a chance to look at the dead brother. I didn't know before hand what was happening until I saw him. It was the most gruesome thing I had ever seen in my whole lifetime. I was just a kid, and having seen this gruesome thing that people did to others will forever change the way I think about people.

I saw the father and brother laying on the dead man's body sobbing in horror. We never ever imagined that we would see something like this happen to another human being. It was unbearable to watch. The father and son had to bury the dead man's body nearby. We knew then that the Khmer Rouge was still around this area, and we are not too far away from them and the jungle.

The surviving brother explained everything to us since we were closer to him. We were all terrified of what had happened to the man's son. We gathered around in a large group and decided that we must get out of this place because we were not safe there. The Khmer Rouge were scattered somewhere around this area. That's exactly what we did. We left that area and continued to move west. We wanted to stay as far away from the jungle as possible. We kept on moving along for several days, stopping only for short rests.

Chapter 18

We reached the city of Batambong several days later. We noticed there were many people living in this part of the city. We saw many soldiers patrolling the area as we just reached the outskirt. These soldiers were the North Vietnamese soldiers taking over part of our country at that time. Somehow we all were happy to see these Vietnamese soldiers because they actually did us a favor by forcing the Khmer Rouge into the jungle. Although these Vietnamese soldiers were trying to take over part of our country, we didn't care because we just wanted to get away from the Khmer Rouge.

When we got to the outskirt of the city, the Vietnamese soldiers actually left us alone, and we were allowed to settle down there. We saw people out and about selling food and trading things with each other. There were markets near. I remember settling down under this big house surrounded by big sand bags. That was where we chose to stay at least for a little while. Everyone else found his or her own little spot to stay. There was another family that decided to stay with us under this house.

We used the sand bags as our beds at night. Mom still had a

little left over rice that we helped carry from the last place and we lived off that for a short time. We didn't have any blankets or anything like that to cover our bodies at night; thank god the weather in Cambodia is warm through out the year. Sometimes at night it gets a little chilly, but nothing compared to the cold weather in America.

One rainy night while sleeping under this house on the sand bags, I was bitten by something and it hurt badly. I started to scream the minute that it bit me, and that woke up my mother. She turned around and asked me what had happened? I told her that I was bitten by something, and I wasn't sure what it was, but it hurt like hell. My mother searched for the flashlight and looked around the area to see what had bitten me. As I got up, there was a scorpion running around the sand bag, so my mother killed it with the flashlight. That scorpion had bitten me on my left cheek.

Once my mother killed the scorpion, I went right back to bed because I was so tired. When I woke up the next day, the whole left side of the face was swollen like a balloon and hurting. My mother, sister and brother were freaked out when they saw my swollen face. I was worried that I was going to die from the scorpion bite. My mother was also worried that I might die. She went all over the area asking people what she could do about the scorpion bite. People told my mother there was not a lot she could do about it. They told her I would not die from a scorpion bite, but the swelling takes time to come down.

They also warned my mother that I shouldn't rub or scratch the area of where the scorpion bit me, because that may cause some infection; it would be a problem then. When my mother came back and told me all about what not to do with my face, I didn't even touch it for several days. That was how much the scorpion bite scared me. After a few days the swelling on my face slowly came down. After about four days the swelling was completely gone. I was ecstatic that I was back to normal again.

People were absolutely right that it took time for that swelling to come down as long as I didn't irritate it and make it worse by scratching. Each night from that point on I would look around with the flashlight to make sure there were no scorpions around before I went to bed. If I remembered correctly, the scorpions only came out when it rained because they had nowhere else to go but on the sandbags.

Those sandbags may have made them feel comfortable, giving them a place to hide out, just like we used the sand bags as our beds. A scorpion never bit me again, even though we all had seen more scorpions during the day around the sand bags. We killed all we saw; it was strange! Maybe the scorpions also sleep at night.

We decided to stay under this house for a while because we didn't know where to go quite yet or who to trust in this part of the city. With all the sand bags around us, it seemed a little safer there, except we had to look out for those black scorpions. Actually, the black scorpions never bit anyone else after me. I was bitten by one and survived; it wasn't that bad.

We all laid low under this big house. My mother was the only one going out during the day to trade things for food. Each morning my mother would take a couple of small cans of rice to the market for the exchange. Sometimes she would bring back cooked rice, and sometimes she would bring back noodles and other goods. There were people selling and trading things on the side of the street and also in the market place nearby. My mother told us she preferred to go to the market because she thought it was safer than dealing with people on the street. My mother was a business woman in our country, so going out to talk with people and wheel and deal for the best transaction was her thing, and she loved doing it. When we first got to this part of the city we knew right away that it would provide my mother good opportunities to do better, and we in turn would continue to survive this ordeal.

We had just enough food to eat each day to get by, and we were lucky to be away from the Khmer Rouge for the time being. We had just enough left over raw rice to trade up for other food. By this time we had eaten all the dried rats.

One morning my mother took off with some rice in a small bag to exchange in the market, but she never returned home that day. By evening, we were all very worried about my mother's safety. We thought she could not have gotten lost because she had always returned home in the evening. By that evening, my sister, my brother and I went out and around the area to ask people if they had seen my mother? We described her age and appearance to the people. We asked everybody we saw if they had seen our mother, but no one knew anything or had an answer for us.

When it got dark that night, we had to come back to the place where we were staying at to sleep. The people next to us were also concerned about my mother's safety. We thought the Khmer Rouge might have somehow captured her. The North Vietnamese soldiers always left us alone, and there was no reason for my mother to get lost; she had done this everyday. As worried as we all were that night, we went to sleep without eating because mom didn't come home from the market. All we had was some raw rice left over from earlier in the day, and we were too worried about mom to eat.

Although we tried to go to sleep that night, we couldn't sleep much at all because mom wasn't around. We might have gotten a few hours of sleep before the sunrise. We all sat under the house on the sand bags the next day just waiting to see if mom was ever going to come back. We were all fearful of what had happened to her.

It was not until that evening that our mother returned. We were so happy to see her. We told her that, when she didn't come back the day before, we thought we had lost her to the Khmer Rouge again. We asked her why she didn't come home the day before and what had happened to her. How could she just leave us alone by ourselves? She told us on her way back from the market, a few Vietnamese soldiers captured her and took her to the nearby jail. Basically they saw my mother was wheeling and dealing in the market and thought that she had some gold or something like that with her and decided to capture her. They asked my mother many questions while she was in jail that night.

She told the Vietnamese soldiers that all she did was exchange raw rice for other food to bring home for her children. She told us that the Vietnamese soldiers were looking for gold; that's why they had to take her away. Since my mother didn't have any gold with her that day, they decided to keep her one night in jail and release her the next day.

My mother also told us that she was scared that night and worried a lot while she was in jail because she wasn't sure what those soldiers was going to do to her. She thought she wasn't going to see us any time soon. She was, however, very lucky that they decided to let her go the next day. My mother believed that those soldiers that captured her didn't care about what she did with the exchanges and trades. They were just looking for gold. She did not understand why they were looking for gold. When my mother came back, she also had fried noodles for all of us to eat. Honestly we thought we had lost her to the Khmer Rouge. It scared us terribly that she all of a sudden disappeared for the day and night. It was really strange! After my mother was released from the Vietnamese jail, she felt that we would be a little safer if we went deeper into the city to find a place to stay.

My mother was a very smart person, and would always be out and about every morning looking around the city, talking to people and exchanging things with them. She would always ask the most sincere and knowledgeable person around where the safest place to settle down in the city was. She could actually read people. An honest man had told her that it was safer for all of us to find a better place to live instead of under the house.

A few days later, we told the people next to us that we were going to try to find a better place to live. The next day we all said goodbye to our neighbors; they were nice people, who decided to stay where they were. We got all of our stuff, including some leftover rice, and left this part of the city behind. We walked for hours to try and find a new home. It was a big city and we felt safe with the Vietnamese soldiers around. As long as they were around, the Khmer Rouge was not, and that was good for us.

We searched many hours for a new place to stay within the city. Finally we got to this building where people were living in one side at the lower level. The other side of the building was left vacant, and that was where we all settled down. There was plenty of room for the four of us to stay in the corner of this building.

My mother decided that we should settle there because it was close to many things. There were a couple of wells nearby where we could get water. One was just about a block away. The market was also nearby where mom could go and do her magic trades and exchanges. This area was also in the middle of the city. My mother told me the actual name of the city was, Swei Si Sappon, or at least it was pronounced that way. My mother felt that it was safer to stay in the middle of the city, where there were a lot of people. If something was to happen, we could follow them.

Vietnamese soldiers patrolled this area, and some even drove their big tanks around the city, waving to us; they were friendly. Behind our new home was a big back yard, filled with dirt and several trees. Mom really liked this building, and she felt safer here more than anywhere else, and we all know that mom knew best when it came to this sort of thing. We didn't have a father to guide us, so mom was our father and mother. Once we had all of our stuff unpacked, we made this building our home for the time being. We all felt comfortable and safe living there. Each day my mother and sister would go to the nearby market to exchange rice for other goods like noodles, cooked rice, fish, clothes, etc. I don't know how my mother and sister did their work, but after a few weeks of living there, they actually gained more rice by trading at the market everyday. It was like my mother and sister had gained rice profits instead of money. At that time raw rice was worth as much as money for some odd reason.

After several weeks of constantly going to the market, wheeling and dealing to exchange for raw rice, my mom and sister had a bag full. The full bag of rice we had was valuable!

We could exchange it by the cup for anything we wanted. Each morning my brother and I would each take a cup of rice to the market and exchange it for a big bowl of noodle soup or a bowl of rice with cooked meat in it. That would be our morning meal. Rice worked great as means of exchange.

Chapter 19

The year was 1978; we had lived in this city for several months. Even though we were surviving better, we knew that one day we would have to get out of this beloved country of ours. Although things were looking good at this time, we knew that things could change at anytime, and no one was safe. We also knew that one day we'd have to escape to Thailand, and eventually to America or Australia, for a better life. While we were still in the city, we'd have to do our best to survive, and the Vietnamese soldiers gave us the opportunity to do just that. We were thankful that they forced the Khmer Rouge into the jungle. We did not, however, agree or accept that they were trying to take over part of our country.

While my mother and sister were out each day in the market exchanging goods, I would go to the well and get water, so mom could cook rice or soup for dinner. I would use two five gallon buckets to get water from the well each morning. I would tie each bucket with a string and hook, one bucket to each end of a sturdy, six-foot stick. Then I carried the buckets, balancing the stick on my shoulders.

Once I got to the well, I filled both five gallon buckets,

using the small bucket provided for this purpose. I carried the buckets home on my shoulders using the six-foot stick. Basically, it was a man's job to tell you the truth, but I had to do it because we needed water each day, and the Khmer Rouge had killed my father and uncle.

After a while, the two five gallon buckets of water became quite heavy, but I always managed to get the water home for my mother and sister to cook with. Sometimes my younger brother would go with me and try to help out, and sometimes he would be with my sister and my mom out in the market.

Several times a week I had to go with the other men riding the cow carriage out of the city to get wood and dry tree branches for mom, so she can use it to start the cooking fire. Sometimes we would ride the cow carriage for several hours one way before we got to the area where we could gather wood and tree branches. It was far away from the city, but it wasn't in the jungle. The people that I went with knew where they were going and where the Khmer Rouge would be. I felt pretty safe with these men.

My mother would pack rice and other things for me to take along and eat. As far as I can remember, I was the only kid that went with the other adults to gather wood. These men would always know exactly where to go. Sometimes it took a while to get to the place we needed to go, but they always managed to find a place that had plenty of dried wood.

Each day that I went with these men, I would gather lots of

wood and tree branches and tie it up in several bunches to take back home. I felt proud for what I was doing for the family. There were no other kids that wanted to do what I did then. We would go to get wood at least twice a week, and it would last a long time, even though we used a lot to make fire. Each week, we would have left over wood. I ended up stacking this in the back of the building for later use.

I was a very busy kid, with many chores each day. While my mom and sister were out in the market doing their exchanges and trades, I took my brother with me, along with a couple cans of rice, to trade it for cooked noodles in the morning so we could have something to eat.

That would only happen sometimes when my mom and sister were too busy. Usually my sister was the one to take my brother out to get food from the market. We often exchanged goods with the Vietnamese soldiers because they were always around patrolling that area of the city. We were lucky that they were nice to us and wanted to exchange stuff for cooked rice or chicken. These Vietnamese soldiers were hungry and always needed foods.

My mother would always try to help these Vietnamese soldiers out by giving them cooked rice when they were around our area. That made them feel thankful and comfortable around us, and later on they would bring live chicken to trade up with my mother for cooked rice and other food. After talking with these soldiers and getting to know them, my mother learned a little bit of the Vietnamese language. My mother was a quick learner whenever she put her mind to it; so learning Vietnamese came easy for her. She was a natural.

Since we had a big yard in the back of the building and I loved animals, especially chickens and roosters, I asked my mother if she could buy or trade for a few chickens so I could raise them. My mother thought that was a good idea and agreed to get me a few chickens, but only if I promised to take care of them. I told her that I had taken care of many cows and buffalo before, and they were huge animals, so chickens should be no problem. It would be fun and easy to care for them.

Since my mother had befriended the Vietnamese soldiers and had been trading with them and helping with food, before I knew it she had brought home a few chickens and a rooster. These chickens came from the Vietnamese soldiers who had traded them for the rice from my mother. I had no idea where these soldiers got the chickens from, but my guess was that they got them from the market or maybe from the farm somewhere. I didn't care how or where they got the chickens from. I just wanted those chickens so I could take care of them.

Anyway, I was very happy that mom got these chickens for me to care for. Raising them kept me very busy, but I took very good care of those chickens.

We had plenty of rice while living in the city because my mom and my sister had done a great job of trading things for it.

Each day I would feed my chickens rice, and they loved it.

All I had to do was throw some rice out on the yard, and they all came rushing in to eat it. Feeding the chickens was simple. After a few months, the hen and the rooster must have mated because the hens laid some eggs in the dirt out back. I was surprised and quite happy that they actually laid eggs.

I gave the eggs to my mother, who was also very surprised. From that point on, we had eggs to eat, and that was a good thing. The hens would take turns laying more eggs.

Several weeks later, we had baby chicks in addition to the chicken. I never thought that chickens could lay that many eggs and have so many babies, but they did. It was incredible to witness the eggs being hatched. I really enjoyed raising these chickens by myself because it was so much fun watching the chicks hatch from eggs and then grow into chickens. After a while there were so many chickens, that we ended up eating many of them.

Sometimes mom would take some chickens to the market and trade them in for other food, clothing and sometimes even for gold. I did all the killings because I was the only man in the house at the time and my little brother was way too young for that. Looking back now, I feel horrible about killing some of those chickens. It broke my heart then too, but I didn't have any other choices; we had to eat.

The way I killed these chickens was very cruel. To get them ready for killing, I would first select the chicken we wanted and crossties wings together so it could not move around or try to run away. Then I removed all of the hairs from its necks. I then put a small bowl under the chicken's neck while, holding it down with both of my legs. I took a knife out and cut the chicken's neck about half an inch across the area where I had removed all the hairs. Then I would drain all the blood from the chicken's neck into the small bowl.

Once the chicken was dead, I put it in a big pot of boiling water. That way I could remove all of its feathers more easily. After a few minutes in the boiling water, I removed the chicken from the pot. I proceeded to pluck off all of the feathers. I then gave it to my mom and sister so they could cut it up and cook it.

We also cooked the chicken's blood that I've saved in the small bowl. Most of the time we used the chicken's blood to make soup rice for breakfast the next day. I know it sounds awful and very bad, but that was the way we had to live. We survived by eating pretty much anything. I must have killed hundreds of chickens in all during our short time in the city.

I remember we had two good-sized roosters, and they were very healthy and well fed. One of the roosters I called my prize rooster. Sometimes I would take my prize rooster to go cock fighting. I would sharpen both of its spurs. My prize rooster had thick long spurs. Once I sharpened the spurs, it was ready to fight. I would tie a long string to the rooster's right leg and carry the string with me just in case it got in trouble during the fight, then I could pull it away from the other rooster.

I usually took my rooster out around the neighborhood to

look for other roosters. Whenever my rooster saw a worthy opponent, he would let me know he wanted to fight by flaring his neck hairs. I then let him go while still holding on to the long string in my hand. The fight looked so very cool to me then, the way the roosters would jump at each other with their neck hairs flaring. After a while the loser would try to run away; that's when I knew the fight was over.

Sometimes the fight would be bloody because of the spurs that they have on their legs. They would cut each other up in the head and body. My rooster would win 90% of the time that I took him out to fight because it was a strong, healthy and well-fed rooster. I took great pride in that prize rooster. I always sharpened its spurs to keep him in tiptop condition. He was my favorite rooster, and even the few times he lost a fight, he was still very strong when I took him home. I guess I was a bad kid when it came to this sort of thing.

My daily activities and chores consisted of getting water from the well in the morning, feeding the chickens, and taking a few cans of rice to trade for noodle soup in the market. When necessary, I took my brother with me in the morning to get noodle soup when my mom and sister were too busy. In the evening, my job was to kill a few chickens so mom could prepare them for dinner. Once the sunset or whenever it got dark, I would gather all the chickens in the backyard and put them in their cage. Some would sleep on the tree branches because there wasn't enough room in the cage.

Several times a week, I would go out with the men to gather wood and tree branches. Whenever I had time, I would take my prize rooster out and have a cockfight with another rooster nearby. Those were my daily activities. Sometimes I would take my brother with me to get water in the morning because he wanted to go and sometimes because my mom and sister were too busy at the market.

One fateful day, I took my brother with me to get well water and something horrible happened. That day I decided to go get water from the well near our place. Usually we would go to the well that was farther from our building because it had more water, but that day there were way too many people in line. The well that was closer to where we live had less water coming out of it, but we didn't have to wait for anybody. Anyway, when we got to the well near our place, I noticed that most of the well water was gone, except one area in the middle of the well at the bottom, where some water has leaked out from the side. I told my brother we should just get water from this well, since we were already there. We might have to wait a few minutes in between each bucket, but it shouldn't take too long. Basically, the well was dried out except for that little bit in the middle.

This well must have been at least ten feet deep. On top of the well there was a log running across the center with a rope hanging down from the middle where people could tie their bucket, roll it down and get the well water. To the side of the log there was a handle like a steering wheel, so people could roll the bucket of water back up. I had done this many times before, so I knew how to get water from the well.

When I rolled up the bucket of water from the well, I had to turn around and walk a few feet to dump it into my own bucket. As I walked away from the well, my brother somehow got on the center of the log that was placed on the well and was hanging in the middle of it looking down at the bottom of the well. I saw fear in his eyes as I turn around to look at him, and he had asked me to help him get off the log. I saw that my brother was about to fall into the well. I told him to stay still so I could go get some help because I didn't think I could pull him from the log by myself.

The log was unstable and made to roll around so people could get water up from the well. As soon as I walked a few steps away, I saw my brother fall. I ran to the well and looked. I saw my brother just lying motionless at the bottom bleeding from the head. I tried to call his name many times, but he did not answer me. He was unconscious and bleeding pretty badly.

I thought my brother was dead. Although he was lying in the bottom of the well, his head did not touch the water. I left him there and ran back home for help. When I got home, my mom and my sister were still out at the market, so I went to look for them. When I found my mother and sister, I told them what happened. My mother was shaken with fear that my brother might die, so she asked a few men to come help. My mother was yelling and screaming because she was scared of what might happen to my brother.

When we got back to the well, my brother was still lying there. One of the two men had a ladder with him and proceeded to lower it down the well. When my mother saw my brother lying there bleeding from his head and motionless, she lost it and broke down crying. She actually almost pushed one of the men down the well. She worried that my brother might die. All I heard my mother say to this man was "hurry up! Go down there and get my son back up," over and over again. He was trying as fast as he could.

A few minutes later he emerged from the well with my brother on his shoulders. My brother was still unconscious and had a big gash on his head in the same spot he cracked it open falling off the ladder months earlier. By this time, there were a lot of people around trying to help. I remember this lady putting some kind of homemade medicine on my brother's head to stop the bleeding. There were no other medicines available; that was all she had with her. Then she put a piece of tape over my brother's head to secure it. The homemade medicine was somewhat like the one that had been used on my brother's head when he first fell from the hut about a year earlier.

This homemade medicine really worked. A few minutes after it had been spread on my brother's head, the bleeding stopped. A short time later, my brother regained consciousness, but he was barely moving. When he opened his eyes to look at my mother, she was relieved and very thankful that so many people had come to my brother's rescue. At this time, I felt very guilty that my brother fell down the well. I was there too and couldn't prevent the accident. I had no idea why my brother was climbing on that log. Maybe he thought that was a fun thing to do at the time. What he didn't know was that the log was unstable and could roll around.

He was also very lucky that the well was dry with only a little bit of water that was in the center. He was also fortunate that his head did not land in the center of the well, or he would have drowned. After my brother became conscious again, we took him home and cared for him until he had completely recovered from the injury.

We all thought that god might have looked out for my brother because he had survived falling down the deep well. If another person would have fallen down the same well, there's no question that person would have die. Anyway, a few weeks later, with lots of tender loving care from all of us, my brother had completely recovered from the fall, but he was never allowed back to the well again. Actually that was a relief for me too, because that way I didn't have to worry about my brother getting into mischief while I was trying to get water. From then on, my brother had to go with my mother and sister.

Chapter 20

By this time, my mother was seriously thinking about trying to escape from our country to our neighbor Thailand if the opportunity arose. We did not want to get caught when all of the fighting started again. In the meantime, my mother continued to barter rice for money and gold at the market because she believed that, in the long run, it was worth a lot more than rice. My mother warned all of us to be prepared and had everything planned out in the event of an escape from Cambodia to Thailand. I remember seeing some of the gold my mother had sewed in the seam of each of our pants and shirts to hide it from people.

My mother knew that if we were to escape, we might run into other people, maybe even thieves or bad people who would want to rob us. Hiding some of the gold in the seam of each of our pants and shirts was an excellent idea. Each of our pants and shirts was prepared with gold running along the seam, unnoticeable to the human eye. I thought it was very clever of my mother to get ready for when we had an opportunity to escape. We wanted to escape without people knowing we had lots of gold with us.

My mother would go out and talk to different people everyday about opportunities to escape to Thailand. She wanted to take the three of us to Thailand and eventually to either America or Australia where we would have a better life. She always mentioned her interest in escaping Cambodia to the people whom she could trust, hoping that some day some one would help her accomplish her goal.

The year was 1979, and we were still living in the city but desperately wanted to get out of Cambodia. Even though we were doing better without the Khmer Rouge, we also knew that living in Cambodia would not give us a chance at a good future. Although the Khmer Rouge was forced away from the city to the jungle and mountain by the North Vietnamese soldiers, we knew that one day there would be fighting again and we would get caught in it. No one would be safe living in Cambodia. We didn't know what would happen the next day.

One fateful day, my mother came home with the news that she had found someone who knew of other people who could help us escape to Thailand, but we had to pay them either money or gold to get us there. They would accept either. My mother also told us that if we were to escape with these people, for safety it would have to be at night, probably around midnight. We would not escape during the day; my mother had been told that it was far too risky.

When my mother heard that there were people who could help us escape from Cambodia to Thailand, she couldn't wait to tell all of us. When we heard the good news, we were all very happy and excited but also fearful, not knowing what could happen during the escape. We did not want to be captured, especially by the Khmer Rouge.

So my mother agreed to meet with the people who would secretly help us escape to Thailand. I believed these people were Thai Wardens or soldiers who knew the roads between Cambodia and Thailand and also knew how to read maps of the jungle. My mother then set up a date and time when we all would meet.

Once my mother had met with these people, the date and time had been set for us to meet with the Thai Wardens. We would meet them right before midnight. Mom had also told us that we would be escaping with a few other families who also wanted to go to Thailand. When my mother got back from meeting with these people, we immediately packed all of our stuff in small bags. I remember trading most of our chickens for gold and some money so we could pay the Wardens. My mother didn't tell anyone about our plan; it was too dangerous. After trading most of the chickens and everything else too, including rice and some clothing that we couldn't take with us, we were all ready to go. We just waited for the date and time to leave.

On the day before we were scheduled to meet with the Wardens, mom had each one of us wear the gold-filled shirts and pants. She told each of us to never ever take it off for any reason because we might lose them. The gold that mom had sewed on each one of our shirts and pants were worth a lot of money, and if we were to lose it, we would be in big trouble. The next night, we were fully prepared to leave Cambodia. We prayed that our journey to Thailand would be safe and trouble free.

Right before midnight we met with the Wardens. My mother and a few other families who would be escaping with us had an agreement with the Wardens that we would pay them once we all crossed the border and into Thailand. Once all of that has been settled and agreed upon, we took off at exactly midnight. We followed the Wardens who lead us through the jungle.

The escape was treacherous, and we walked so many miles through the rough jungle of Cambodia. We were fearful of getting caught by the Khmer Rouge in the mine-filled jungle between Cambodia and Thailand. We all knew that the Khmer Rouge was still somewhere in the jungle, and if we took the wrong way we might run into them and will be killed.

The Thai Wardens claimed they knew all the roads in the jungle and knew exactly where the Khmer Rouge would be. They assured us we would not run into them if we all kept very quiet during our escape and followed them precisely. We had no choice but to trust them. I recall crossing one river during our escape with a small banana boat that the Thai Wardens had set up for us. At least twelve of us, including the Wardens, had to ride in the small banana boat.

The boat barely floated on the river because there were so many people on it. The water on the river was almost the same level as the very top of the banana boat, and if one person were to rock the boat, it would sink immediately. Many of the people on the boat did not know how to swim, including my sister, brother and a few others. We all took a big risk crossing the river on this little boat across the river, but we wanted badly to escape. There was no turning back once we got on the river. If the boat were to sink, we all probably would have drowned.

As the Wardens paddled forward, we all sat very still, holding each other tight so the boat wouldn't rock sideways. We didn't even talk to one another during the boat ride across the river. We were afraid to make any noises at all because it might rock the boat, if that make any sense. We were all very lucky to have made it across the river in that overcrowded boat. Once we made it across the river to the other side, we got out slowly, one by one, until we were clear of the boat. The Thai Wardens told us to be absolutely quiet as we proceeded to walk through the jungle, because there might be some Khmer Rouge around. We entered the jungle part of the country and the most dangerous part of our escape. We were afraid the young kids, including my brother, might get scared and cry.

As we continued on foot, we heard gunshots in the air and bombs going off, and we could see the flames and smoke in the sky. As we traveled through the jungle, the bombs and gunshots would go off in a series, stopping for a while, and then going off again. This lasted throughout the night. We walked through thorn bushes and over uneven ground. We repeatedly fell down and got up. Although these thorn bushes cut us all, we had to keep quiet. This took a lot of energy, and we were all very tired and scared, not knowing when the bombs would hit us or when we would step on a landmine.

Once the gunshots, grenades and bombings stopped, it became quiet again for a short time. The Thai Wardens whispered to us, "be very quiet and move slowly." It was very frightening to hear all the bombs and grenades that went off so close by. You had to be there to experience the horror! I guess the Thai Wardens were afraid that if the kids made any noises after the bombings had stopped, the Khmer Rouge hear and come after us. At one point my brother and a few other kids were either scared or hungry, and they started to cry after the bombings stopped, so my mother and the other parents put their hands over the children's mouths to prevent them from making noises.

Tired from running and walking through the jungle, we came to a resting place somewhere near these big trees. We heard the voices of the Khmer Rouge yelling not too far away. We covered my brother's mouth with our hands as we shook with fear. Then the Thai Wardens whispered at us again, "we must continue to move through the jungle or the Khmer Rouge will catch up with us." We did not get to rest very long and had to keep on moving with the Wardens who were trying very hard to help us. From the sound of their voices, the Khmer Rouge was nearby.

The bombs, grenades and gunshots continued again after a brief stop. The bombings continued periodically. The Khmer Rouge was trying to fight back the North Vietnamese. We didn't know for sure what was happening, but we just kept on moving with the Thai Wardens.

We've made it through one part of the jungle and came to a village where we saw other people running away from the bombings. We could see all the smoke and fire from the grenades and the bombs. We were all terrified of the sound and the fire that filled the sky. We thought we were going to be hit with one of these bombs for sure because it was getting louder and louder.

We came to a stop at one of the houses in this village because we were too exhausted to move any further, and we didn't care whether or not we were with the bombs. We rested in this house for a few minutes and there were no one there beside us in this house. People had abandoned it and left for good.

We had no idea where the other people were headed, but we continued to stick with the Thai Wardens who had helped us to this point. After a few minutes of rest, we started following the Wardens through another part of the jungle. By this time, the night became almost morning, and we started to see a little bit of daylight as we continued forward. The Thai Wardens told us that we were getting closer to the Thai border and should get there soon if we kept on moving.

Everyone was exhausted from walking and running through

the jungle for at least seven hours without any food to eat or drink. All we wanted was to get to the border of Thailand. Morning came and we could finally see each other more clearly. We had walked and run for many miles through the jungle and gotten away from the bombings. We also made it through without stepping on land mines that the Khmer Rouge had planted throughout the jungle, which I found amazing. The Thai wardens certainly knew their way around the jungle and mountains between Cambodia and Thailand.

We walked through some thick bushes and long grass and up the hill as we crossed through the last part of the jungle. We came up to a roadside, where the Wardens told us we'd reached the Thai border, and a truck will come by soon to pick us up and take us to the refugee camp. We were all ecstatic to have made it to the Thai border without stepping on land mines and getting caught by the Khmer Rouge. It was an incredible escape through the jungle and mountain filled with land mines.

I remember a funny incident once we have reached the Thai border. My brother started to cry because he was so hungry and tired. He had told my mother that he wanted to go back to where we came from. My brother tried to run back down the hill, but my mother grabbed a hold of him just in time. He continued to cry for about five minutes that he wanted to go back to Cambodia as my mother held him in her arms.

It didn't matter now how loud my brother was crying because we all have made it to Thailand and were far away from the Khmer Rouge. We all felt safe now. My mother continued to explain to my brother that we could not go back to our country. We had made it to Thailand and we would be in camp soon; then we could eat. She told him we would be much safer in Thailand, and it would be way too far to try to go back.

She kept on telling my brother to calm down and that we would have food soon. Finally, my mother explained that if we were to go back, we would step on one of the bombs that the Khmer Rouge planted along the jungle and would be killed immediately. That scared my brother, and he immediately stopped crying and became calm and quiet again. I thought it was hilarious for my brother to do this, especially when we had already made it to Thailand.

We were very thankful that the Thai Wardens really knew their way around the jungle. If they didn't, we would have been killed during the escape, either by running into the Khmer Rouge or stepping on the land mines. The Thai wardens were nice to all of us. They sat along the roadside with us as we waited for the truck. We were all very hungry and tired, with absolutely no energy left as we all lay down at the side of the road waited for our ride. The Wardens wouldn't get paid until the truck arrived. We waited at least an hour on the Thai border before the small Toyota pickup came by to pick us up. Once the truck got there, we all climbed in the back. My mother and a few other families who were with us, had to pay the Thai Wardens. I had no idea how much my mother paid them for taking us to Thailand, but I'm sure it was a lot of money. We thanked them for their help in getting us safely into Thailand, and then we said goodbye.

We barely fit into the back of the small Toyota pick up, but we managed to get everyone in. We were just so happy and thankful that we all had made it alive. It was a miracle that we all have made it and no one was hurt or killed. Looking back, I can hardly believe it. God must have been on our side.

Chapter 21

I remember a great sense of freedom as we rode on the back of that Toyota truck along the Thailand road. Even though my mother, sister, brother and I were hungry and tired, the minute that we got on that truck, we all had smiles on our faces knowing that we were free from the Khmer Rouge. The truck was driven by anther Thai Warden who was connected to the two Wardens who had helped us escaped from Cambodia. He had to stop at a gas station to fill up on his way to drop us at the refugee camp.

There was a small market at this gas station where my mother bought some bags of instant noodles with the money that she had saved up. Basically she exchanged the Cambodian money for Thai money and bought the box of instant Asian Kung Fu noodles. I remember counting the bags of noodles; there were thirty great tasting bags in that box.

We were so hungry that when mom brought the noodle for us, we each immediately opened a bag and started eating it raw because there were no places to cook them. The noodles were crunchy and tasted amazingly delicious. We must have eaten at least four bags each. The word "hungry" was an under statement. My mother also bought some water at this gas station market because we desperately needed it too. The Warden who drove the Toyota truck was nice enough to give us a long break so we could eat our noodles and drink some water before taking off again.

When everyone was finished eating and back on the back of the truck, we took off again riding proudly in the back. To me it was a fun ride. Because the truck didn't have a canopy, I could see all of the views of the Thai roads and trees and other vehicles along the way. I believe everyone else thought it was a fun ride too because we were all talking to each other and smiling. A few hours later, we reached the refugee camp and the Warden dropped us off. This camp was called Sakeo, and a barbwire fence surrounded it. We were greeted by Thai soldiers who gave us a tent to stay in, or something similar to that. Our bed was a flat piece of wood, but it was comfortable enough for the moment.

We could not get out to go anywhere outside of the camp area because Thai soldiers guarded it day and night. There was a big gate at the main entrance locking all of us in the camp. We had to be inside this camp at all times unless they told us otherwise. There were many other refugees in this camp.

Even though we were locked in, they did provide us some decent food to eat. Many Cambodian refugees lived in this camp, and most of them had escaped from Cambodia the same way we did. If someone tried to get out, they would be in big trouble with the Thai guards. The camp was very dusty, especially when the trucks that brought the food came in. They would drop us food twice a day, once in the morning and again in the evening. They would give us rice and fish and sometimes pork, which was a lot better than what the Khmer Rouge gave us in Cambodia. Also, we felt safe in Thailand, even though they wouldn't let us out of the camp. We didn't care; we had food!

We no longer had to worry about the Khmer Rouge torturing us or trying to kill us. Basically what we had to do when the food truck came in was to run to where it would stop and line up because it was first come first serve. I would always run when I saw the food truck enter the gate, getting there early for the rice and fish they handed out.

Each one of us had to line up because they gave each person enough food for one family. All of the water was provided in a big tank, so we were never short of water. Once in a while the water would run low, but we were never out. After living in this camp for about two months, we were told to move to another camp somewhere in Thailand called Mi Rut. The big bus came to pick us up when it was time to go. We were randomly picked to move.

Mi Rut was a much nicer camp, where we were given a little more freedom to roam around. The same basic food was offered to us, but while we were in this camp, we were also allowed to exchange and buy food from Thai people outside the barbwire fences if you had the money. We were not allowed to go outside the camp to exchange goods with the Thai people, and they were not allowed to come into the refugee camp.

We were not allowed to exchange for anything else besides food and, sometimes the amount was limited because the Thai soldiers were there all the time, keeping an eye on who was doing what around the camp. Most of the time we just exchanged rice and stuff for watermelons. I thought they did this just to help us out as refugees because the weather was incredibly hot every day. Sometimes the Thai soldiers would run those people out of the camp area because they caused too much commotion. Most of the time the Thai people, including the soldiers, were very nice to us. After a while, we started learning the basic Thai language from them.

Another good thing about living in this second refugee camp was that they allowed us to play at the nearby beach several times a week. They also allowed us to go shopping in Bangkok once a month. The bus to Bangkok would come and pick us up once a month to take us shopping if we wished.

That was like heaven to us, getting away from the refugee camp once a month to just roam around the city and, if we had the money, to shop. There was a time limit, several hours I believe, for how long we could shop in Bangkok. None of us had any problem with the time limit, because we didn't have that much money anyway. I remember my mother would always buy stuff to take back to the camp, and sometimes she even bought electronic toys for my brother and me. She even exchanged gold for money there in the city.

We would often go to the beach and swim with the other refugees, and we always had fun. There were coconut trees all around the beach area, and I remember climbing them to pick the coconuts. We ate them before going out for a swim.

We were allowed to go to the beach twice a week. It was our way of relieving stress caused by being locked up in the crowded camp.

We were also offered schooling. My mother thought that was a great opportunity for our family, so she sent me to the school to learn the Cambodian language, math, and English. That was exactly what I wanted to do as well. I knew for sure that I wanted to learn English because I had a passion for it. I wanted to communicate with Americans when they come in to camp. My sister also took a few Cambodian and English classes. An American and Cambodian teacher taught it there. My brother was too young, and they did not have classes for kids that young in this refugee camp. I tried my very best to learn both languages at the same time. It was challenging but I also found it rewarding.

Whenever I came back home from the classroom, I was allowed to go play around the camp area with other kids, but only after I had first eaten lunch. I was very passionate about learning English because my mother had told us that our main goal in escaping Cambodia was to eventually go to America. So whenever I saw Americans walking around the refugee camp, I would immediately run after each one of them and try to speak the little bit of English I had learned in the classroom. Most of the time I would start out by saying something like hello "my name is Bunthong" and "how are you doing?" The Americans were always impressed that I was trying to speak with them. Sometimes the American people would be riding in the food trucks with the Thai people, and the minute I saw them, I would get excited and could not wait to go up and speak with them. I usually ran after the truck until it stopped, so I could say hello. Once I got to speak with them in English, I was satisfied. I would also get food from them. The food was tossed from the truck to each person who waited in line. I was always in line first because I wanted to get the food and say hello to people in English.

Learning the English language was difficult, but I was willing to start early because I was passionate about it from the beginning. I've kept all of the schoolbooks and notebooks of what I learned there in the refugee camp. I even have all homework. I have several Cambodian and English textbooks, including mathematic and the English language. The English language taught in this refugee camp was basic, but it gave me a head start.

Americans often visited the camp, and most of them were news people with cameras on them. Some of the other Americans were there to help hand out food.

We were also offered a nighttime movie to watch at least several times a month. They were drive-in type movies, usually Cambodian, but occasionally Thai and Chinese as well. We all got to watch the movies whenever they show them at night. We did appreciate all the things the Thai people and the American people did for us while we live in this camp.

We knew while living in this camp that we eventually wanted to be sponsored to go to America, but we did not know anybody who could do this for us. My mother's first priority was to bring all of us to America. She believed it would give us the best chance of a good future, but since we didn't know anybody that would be willing to sponsor us to America; we were willing to go to Australia. My mother knew for sure that we had two uncles in Australia who could sponsor us, if we could find a way to contact them and let them know that we were here living in the Thai refugee camp.

There was a bulletin board in the middle of the refugee camp area where each day people from different countries looking for family and friends posted pictures and letters with their names on them. The bulletin board would be filled with the identities of people's loved ones looking for them. We would go to this place each day to check if any member of our families had survived Cambodia and made it to America before us, and also to check and see if our two uncles from Australia were looking for us. Many people had found their families and friends from different countries through this bulletin board, and they ended up getting sponsored by them to immigrate to those countries.

That bulletin board was a great idea, and it gave us hope to go to it each day and try and find our own families and friends. Then one fateful day, my mother went to the bulletin board just to look and saw this American man holding out a picture of a man and asking the people around if anybody knew him. This man who held the picture up was tall, and the picture was kind of high up, so my mother could not take a good look at it. My mother politely asked the tall American to lower the picture down so she could see it more clearly. The tall man responded and brought the picture closer to my mother so she could take a look at the picture too. As soon as my mother had a chance to look at the picture, she started to yell out loud that the picture was her brother. She asked the American, "How did you get this picture?" The man told my mother he was a Channel Two news anchorman from America, and his name was Stan Wilson. He was on special assignment.

He explained to my mother that her brother, Eng Lim, had contacted him right before he was ready to leave for Thailand and gave him the picture and letter, asking him to try to find his sister and other family members.

By this time my mother had her friend, who spoke good English interpret for her. My mother was so excited and happy that her brother was alive and actually made it to America first that she almost passed out. She thought that my uncle died in Cambodia when the Khmer Rouge took over, because they had killed most of our family members.

After Mr. Wilson explained to my mother through the interpreter that her brother was alive and living in the United States, she broke down and shed tears of joy in front of the anchorman and everyone around. Mr. Wilson then reached inside his pants pocket and gave my mother an American fifty-dollar bill and told her she could buy whatever she wanted with it.

My mother was shocked at his generosity. That was a whole lot of money in Thailand. This man never knew us before, and out of his kind heart, he gave us fifty dollars. We could live two months with plenty of food to eat on fifty American dollars. Mr. Wilson then took video shots of all of us in the camp, and also video of my mom crying, so he could take it back to show my uncle in America.

He also promised my mom that as soon as he got back to America he would let my uncle know that she is alive and living in a Thai refugee camp. Stan Wilson then took some pictures of all of us in the refugee camp to take back with him. My mother and all of us were so thankful to have met this anchorman from America who has brought us the great news that my uncle was alive and living in America. Before Mr. Wilson had to leave the refugee camp, my mother asked him to please let her brother know that we really wanted to come to America. He once again assured my mother that he would definitely let my uncle know as soon as he gets back to America.

My uncle was in the military in our country, and he was also a policeman. He left Cambodia right before the Khmer Rouge took over. I believe my uncle knew something was going to happen to our country and decided to leave and come to America first. He took his family and made it to America in 1975. He had made the right decision. He and his family were very lucky. My uncle is the only living older brother my mother had left. The Khmer Rouge had killed most of my mother's family except one nephew and niece who also had survive Cambodia as we found out later on. My two other uncles in Australia were distant relatives.

We thought for sure we were going to Australia, but the minute that we found out that my mother's older brother was living in the United States, our plan changed. We preferred to come to America where we originally wanted to go.

About a month after Mr. Stan Wilson had left the Mi Rut refugee camp, my mother received a letter from my uncle in America stating that he wanted to sponsor all of us to migrate to the United States as soon as possible, and that he was happy to know that we had escaped Cambodia and made it to Thailand. It was a huge accomplishment, and we were very fortunate. He started the sponsorship paper, and we had to wait for several months before everything was completed.

The year was 1980, and we had lived in this Thai refugee camp for approximately seven months. We have been waiting patiently for several months to hear when we would be schedule to leave for America. My uncle had put a lot of effort in trying to sponsor all of us. He did the best he could in speeding up the process.

A few months passed, and we finally heard the good news that all the paperwork had cleared, and we had been accepted to come to America. My mother was so happy when she heard of this great news, and so were the rest of us. We were scheduled to leave Thailand in May of 1980, but before we could leave, we had to move to another Thai refugee camp called Sorin. We had made many friends at Mi Rut and were sorry to leave. We had to say goodbye to each of them before we left. We took many pictures and shed many tears of joy. Of course they were happy that we would be leaving to our new home in America, but it was still sad for them to see us go. We had bonded with these people for many months, and it was like saying goodbye to family. I also had met a few good friends while staying in this Thai refugee camp and we took pictures together before we said good bye. It was sad to say good bye to my best friend who I had bonded with while living in this camp, but I had to leave with my family.

The bus picked us up from Mi Rut and dropped us off in Sorin, the third and final camp we lived in. We stayed at Sorin for several more months until our scheduled date to fly out of Thailand to the United States. Sorin was clean, and there was no barbwire around it. They provided good food, and we could do pretty much anything we wanted. I guess they knew that we had already been sponsored and were ready to get out of Thailand, so they treated us differently.

On our scheduled date to leave Thailand, the bus came to pick us up from Sorin in the morning and dropped us off at the airport. This was the happiest day of our lives. We knew then we would be forever free from the Khmer Rouge and the sufferings they put us through.

We would be reunited with our uncle and his family who sponsored us to the United States. I remember our flight to America. It was scary and exhilarating at the same time, because it was my first time on a huge airplane. I believe it was a 747 International. We flew from Thailand to Tokyo, from Tokyo to Hong Kong, and from Hong Kong to Seattle. We then flew from Seattle to Portland Oregon, where my uncle and his family awaited us.

When we arrived and got off the plane in Portland, Oregon, my uncle and his family were there to greet us. When my mother saw my uncle for the first time in years, she cried very hard. We all hugged each other for a long time in the airport. I could not explain the feelings I had when we got off the plane. It was like being born again in a new place.

Mr. Wilson and his news crew from Channel Two news were also there to capture the moment. Later that night, he displayed our images on local television. Mr. Wilson saved the videotape of our reunion at the airport and gave it to my uncle later as a keepsake. At the airport, I kept saying to my mother, "don't cry. You are always crying like this again and again." It was captured on the videotape. It didn't matter to my mother; she kept on crying because she said they were tears of joy. I was just embarrassed that other people were staring at us in the airport. It was bad enough that our clothes were ragged, but on top of that mom was crying her heart out in front of all the people and the news crew. If you see the video tape, you can hear me telling my mother to stop crying at the airport.

I remember the ride on the freeway from the airport to my uncle's home in his Ford Fairmont station wagon. It was the most awesome feeling! A feeling of being free…

None of us will ever forget our journey from our homeland, Cambodia, to The United States of America. We endured so much physical and emotional pain, heartaches, and resentments from the Khmer Rouge, but we made it through it all with much luck along the way. My mother, sister, my brother and I had survived Cambodia and the Khmer Rouge Regime. We believe within our hearts that America is the greatest country with the most compassionate people. We know we will have a bright future living in America, the home of the free, the greatest country in the world!

ISBN 1425112854